# DELIGHTFUL

# *Chinese*

# COOKING

by Eng Tie Ang

D1414315

Published by:

## AMBROSIA PUBLICATIONS

Seattle, Washington

Copyright © 1999 by Eng Tie Ang

Requests for permission to reproduce any of the material contained herein should be addressed to:

**Ambrosia Publications**
P.O. Box 30818
Seattle, WA 98103
Phone & Fax (206) 789-3693

Art Direction by Eng Tie Ang
Cover Design by Eng Tie Ang
Cover Production by Shawn Wheeler
Cover Photo by Terry Pagos Photography
Design and Illustrations by Eng Tie Ang and Alex Bissonnette
Food Styling by Veleda Furtado and Eng Tie Ang
Food Styling Assistance by Carla Ferreira and Rose Rentz
Editorial Direction by Donald R. Bissonnette
Typography and Production by Eng Tie Ang
Published by Ambrosia Publications - Seattle, Washington
Printed by Publishers Press - Salt Lake City, Utah

Printed in the United States of America
First Edition
First Printing - 1999

ISBN: 0-9627810-6-1
Library of Congress Catalog Number: 99-94788

# Dedication

With love, thanks, and affection, I dedicate this book to Ang Bun Pit and Kang Siu Tjen, my father and mother, for all that they taught me and their support of me over the years in my efforts to become a successful author.

# On The Cover

1. Eight Treasure Rice Pudding, page 139
2. Lotus Salad, page 57
3. Fried Shrimp Wontons, page 28
4. Crispy Roast Duck, page 122
5. Potstickers, page 31
6. Ginger Sauce, page 15
7. Asparagus with Baby Corn, page 63
8. Hot Hoisin Sauce, page 16
9. Chinese Pancakes, page 25
10. Long-Grain White Rice, page 129

# Table of Contents

# Acknowledgements

I would like to thank many people for their help, support, and encouragement in putting this book together. First, I would like to thank those who helped in the editing process: Debbie Turner, Rose Rentz, and my husband, Donald Richard Bissonnette. I especially owe these people my gratitude for the arduous task of debugging my manuscript and suggesting changes. Second, for giving me suggestions and generously allowing me to use items for the cover photo, I would like to express my appreciation to Nancy Hilty, Veleda Furtado, Dorrienne Chinn, Ashley Chang, Lynn Tungseth, Rose Rentz, Christina Taylor, Jim Wright, Chi Thi Pham, Theresa Christian, Ramona Delgado, and Tilden. Third, for moral and technical support, I would like to thank my mother and father, Kang Siu Tjen and Ang Bun Pit; my brothers, Ang Sen Hoo, Paul Marcius Ang, and Ang Sen Long; my sons, Alex and André Bissonnette; and my friends, Lynn Smith, Christina Taran, Ken LaForce, Celso Galvez, Carla Ferreira, Jasmine Mac, Dana Waters-Beach, Ramona Delgado, Terry Pagos, Lisa Sassi, Hanifa Yahiaoui, Robin Schuy, Dennis Colgan, and Janusz and Malgorzata Mydlarczyk. Finally, I would like to thank all my cooking class students and friends for encouraging me to undertake this project. To all of the above, I offer my sincere thanks and gratitude.

*Eng Tie Ang*
Eng Tie Ang

# Introduction

I always wanted to write a Chinese cookbook, but I kept putting it off for many years because it somehow seemed like the truest test of my knowledge and expertise. It's not that I have ever been afraid to cook any of the specialties in this book. To the contrary, I have cooked them all many times for many years with great success. However, being Chinese, I supposed writing a book about the cooking which I think of as the most sophisticated and wonderful in the world might somehow be presumptuous of me. After all, who am I to be writing about a cuisine that has been in development for five thousand years? What right do I have to presume that I, a mere mortal, can write a cookbook for others on one of China's most important contributions to the world? Well, after years of thinking about it and publishing four other successful cookbooks, I finally decided that I just might be the person to undertake the arduous task of putting together a quick and easy cookbook for others to try their hand at this wonderful cuisine of my heritage. Maybe I had earned the right to publish this cookbook after years of preparation, like the traditional apprentice chefs of China who worked under the supervision of others for decades before finally earning the right to be masters themselves.

For us Chinese, cooking is more than just food preparation for the purpose of feeding our families, friends, guests, and other loved ones. It is the center of most of our social gatherings. It is to be a shared experience, one in which everyone partakes of the pleasure and pride of preparation as well as the enjoyment and delight of eating. It is the bonding agent, or central core, of all our social gatherings. Nothing is planned or carried out without careful consideration of the food which will be consumed to mark the event, whatever it might be. The food will nourish not only the body of those involved in any occasion, but also the spirit of the event itself.

As a very young girl, I remember my mother and other women, alive with motion in the kitchen filled with exotic and mouth-watering aromas, hustling and bustling about with woks crackling, pots steaming, and braziers smoking. Everything was a hubbub of cooking activity and chatter as everyone joined in the frenzied preparation for one feast or another. I was never left as a casual observer though, not in a Chinese household. I was always a part of this activity from my earliest moments. Though a young girl, I was expected to take part, doing whatever little task might be appropriate for one of my age and experience. Everyone older was my mentor and private tutor, giving me instructions, assigning me jobs, and critiquing my results - all for the purpose of training me to one day become the lead cook in my own family and the trainer of those younger and in need of my expertise.

But what is Chinese cooking or Chinese cuisine? What a truly difficult question that is. China has many regional types of cooking, many as different as night and day, but all under the broad category of "Chinese." For example, there is the delicate southeastern cuisine of Canton with its detail to the arrangement and presentation of its dishes so that the natural colors and subtle flavors can be savored both by the palate and the eyes. In contrast, there is Szechwan cuisine from the western part of China with its fiery hot recipes which rely on lots of garlic, chilies, and onions to activate the salivary glands. In northeastern China in the area around Shanghai, one can especially find lots of noodles and cold dishes. In northern China around Beijing, where there is a lot more wheat than rice grown, there are lots of recipes with flour products like Chinese pancakes as well as a heavier reliance on meat and poultry. All of these regional cuisines have over the centuries been mixed together and placed under the name "Chinese" cooking. No matter, however, where one goes or what one eats, the food all has a distinctly "Chinese" character to it and is all wonderful to sample, savor, and enjoy.

Finally, let me mention some changes in these recipes from totally traditional ones. All of these changes are for health reasons. I have attempted to keep fats, oils, eggs, and salt to a minimum wherever possible. Additionally, I have recommended the use of canola oil instead of oils with higher levels of saturated fats. Furthermore, in none of these recipes do I mention the use of monosodium glutamate (MSG). It does add a nice, sweet flavor to many Chinese dishes, but its after-flavor and unhealthy effects make it an ingredient I choose to do without. None of these changes, however, seriously alter the end results in any of the recipes.

# About the Author

Eng Tie Ang was born in Indonesia of Chinese parents, moved to Brazil at the age of five, and came to the United States at the age of twenty-five. She learned cooking at an early age at home and in her parents' small restaurant in Suzano, Sao Paulo, Brazil. Her first and most influential cooking teacher was her mother, a master of many kinds of Oriental cooking. When Ms. Ang was a teenager, she attended a cooking school in her hometown, specializing in Western cooking. In addition to **Delightful Chinese Cooking**, she has also published four other cookbooks: **Delightful Thai Cooking, Delightful Brazilian Cooking, Delightful Tofu Cooking,** and **Delightful Vietnamese Cooking. Delightful Vegetarian Cooking** and **Delightful Italian Cooking** are forthcoming. In addition to her cookbooks, Ms. Ang has also written a children's cultural reader entitled, **The Chinese Lantern Festival**.

When not writing cookbooks, Ms. Ang is a cooking instructor for the University of Washington's Experimental College. She also frequently teaches courses through the Puget Consumers' Co-op, the Seattle Asian Art Museum, and other cooking schools in the Seattle area. She has offered courses in Chinese cooking, Vietnamese cooking, Indonesian cooking, Thai cooking, tofu cooking, vegetarian cooking, Northern Italian cooking, and Brazilian cooking. She also does catering for special events and is a food consultant. Moreover, she is an avid organic gardener and an accomplished batik painter.

Ms. Ang lives in Seattle with her husband, Donald Richard Bissonnette, and two sons, Alex and André.

# CHAPTER ONE

# CONDIMENTS
# &
# SAUCES

# Condiments and Sauces

# AROMATIC FRIED SHALLOTS

**2 cups canola oil**
**10 large shallots, thinly**
**sliced**

Heat the oil in a large wok and deep-fry the shallots for 3 to 5 minutes or until light golden brown and crisp. Drain the shallots on paper towels. Let cool and store in an airtight container. An excellent condiment in soups of all kinds.

*Makes 2 cups.*

# MIXED VEGETABLE PICKLES

**1 large carrot, peeled, thinly**
**sliced**
**1 small white icicle radish**
**(daikon), peeled, thinly**
**sliced**
**1 cucumber, peeled, sliced**
**2 cups water**
**1 cup white vinegar**
**2 tablespoons sugar**
**1 teaspoon salt**
**2 teaspoons Szechwan**
**peppercorns**
**1 fresh red cayenne pepper,**
**thinly sliced**

Combine all the ingredients in a large deep bowl, stir well and marinate the vegetable pickles at least 30 minutes or overnight in a refrigerator. The pickles keep well for at least 5 days in the refrigerator. Serve with any kind of barbecued meat or vegetables.

*Serves 4-6.*

# SZECHWAN CUCUMBER PICKLES

6 pickle cucumbers, peeled,
  sliced diagonally into
  1/2-inch slices
1 tablespoon salt
6 cloves garlic, sliced
2 teaspoons Szechwan
  peppercorns, roasted,
  crushed
2 tablespoons white wine
  vinegar
1 tablespoon sugar
1 tablespoon sesame oil
1 teaspoon hot bean sauce
1 tablespoon Hot Pepper Oil
  (see page 17)
2 fresh red cayenne peppers,
  thinly sliced

Place the cucumbers in a large bowl and mix with the salt. Let stand for 1 hour. Transfer the cucumbers to a colander, then rinse, drain and place them in a large bowl. Add the garlic, peppercorns, vinegar, sugar, sesame oil, bean sauce, Hot Pepper Oil, and peppers. Stir until well blended. Refrigerate for at least 2 hours before serving. They will keep 5 days refrigerated. Serve as a salad or with barbecued meat.

*Serves 4-6.*

# BLACK BEAN SAUCE

2 tablespoons canola oil
2 tablespoons salted black
  beans (Chinese style),
  chopped
1/2 cup water
1/4 cup soy sauce
1/4 cup rice wine

Heat the oil in a small pot and sauté the salted black beans for 1 minute. Add the water, soy sauce, and rice wine and simmer over low heat for 3 minutes. Cool and refrigerate before serving. Serve with fish, eggs or vegetables.

*Makes 1 cup.*

# Garlic Sauce

**juice of 1 large lime**
**4 cloves garlic, minced**
**1 teaspoon sugar**
**1 teaspoon sesame oil**
**3/4 cup soy sauce**

Combine all the ingredients in a small bowl, stir well and refrigerate before serving. Serve with Potstickers (see page 31) or fish.

*Makes 1 cup.*

# Ginger Sauce

**1 tablespoon canola oil**
**4 green onions, chopped**
**1 one-inch piece fresh ginger, peeled and minced**
**3/4 cup light soy sauce**
**3 tablespoons rice vinegar**
**1 tablespoon sugar**

Heat the oil in a small pot and sauté the green onions until light golden brown. Add the ginger, soy sauce, rice vinegar, and sugar. Stir well and simmer over low heat for 1 minute. Cool and serve either warm or cold with barbecued meat, Shao Mai (see page 32), Potstickers (see page 31), or fish.

*Makes 1 cup.*

# HOISIN AND TOMATO SAUCE

1 teaspoon canola oil
1 teaspoon sugar
1 fresh red cayenne pepper,
   chopped
2 tablespoons cornstarch,
   dissolved in 1/4 cup cold
   water
2 tablespoons soy sauce
2 tablespoons hoisin sauce
2 tablespoons ketchup

Mix all the ingredients in a small pot and simmer over low heat for 2 minutes, stirring constantly. Serve with barbecued meat or noodles.

*Makes 1/2 cup.*


# HOT HOISIN SAUCE

1 teaspoon hot bean sauce
1/2 cup canned hoisin sauce
1 tablespoon sugar
1/4 cup water
2 teaspoons sesame oil

Combine all the ingredients in a small bowl, stir well, and refrigerate before serving. Serve with Chinese Pancakes (see page 25), or Crispy Roast Duck (see page 122), or Mu Shu Pork (see page 124).

*Makes 1 cup.*

# HOT MUSTARD SAUCE

6 tablespoons hot mustard
   powder
6 tablespoons water
2 teaspoons rice vinegar or
   white vinegar
2 teaspoons sesame oil

In a small bowl, mix well the mustard powder and water until it forms a smooth paste. Let it stand for 2 minutes. Add the vinegar and sesame oil. Mix well. Serve with Barbecued Pork (see page 23).

*Makes 1/2 cup.*

# HOT PEPPER OIL

2/3 cup canola oil
8 cloves garlic, minced
1/2 cup dried red cayenne
   pepper flakes
1 teaspoon salt

Heat the oil in a small pot and sauté the garlic until light golden brown. Add the cayenne pepper flakes and salt and stir until well blended. Let the mixture cool completely, then pour it into a jar. Serve with meat, fish, or noodles.

*Makes 1 cup.*

17

# LIME SAUCE

juice of 2 limes
1/2 cup sugar
1/2 cup soy sauce
2 fresh red cayenne peppers,
  minced

In a small bowl, combine all the ingredients and stir well until the sugar is dissolved. Serve with barbecued meat or fish.

*Makes 1 cup.*

# PLUM SAUCE

8 dried plums, pitted, soaked,
  drained
juice of 1 lime
1/4 cup water
2 tablespoons sugar
2 fresh red cayenne peppers,
  sliced
2 tablespoons canola oil
3 cloves garlic, minced
1/4 cup canned hoisin sauce

In a blender, blend the plums, lime juice, water, sugar, and cayenne peppers into a smooth sauce. Heat the oil in a small pot, add the garlic, hoisin sauce, and the blended mixture. Stir well and simmer for 2 minutes or until the sauce thickens. Serve with barbecued meat.

*Makes 1 cup.*

# Spicy Black Bean Sauce

1 tablespoon canola oil
2 tablespoons salted black beans (Chinese style), chopped
4 dried red cayenne peppers, chopped
1/2 cup water
1/4 cup soy sauce
1/4 cup hoisin sauce
2 tablespoons ketchup
1 tablespoon sugar
1 teaspoon sesame oil

Heat the oil in a small pot and sauté the salted black beans and cayenne peppers for 1 minute. Add the water, soy sauce, hoisin sauce, ketchup, sugar, and sesame oil. Simmer over low heat for 3 minutes. Cool and serve with meat, fish, crab, or clams.

*Makes 1 cup.*

# Spicy Soy Sauce

1 teaspoon sesame oil
4 fresh red cayenne peppers, minced
1 teaspoon sugar
1/2 cup soy sauce

Combine all the ingredients in a small bowl, stir well, and refrigerate before serving. Serve with barbecued meat or fish.

*Makes 1/2 cup.*

# SWEET AND SOUR SAUCE

1 teaspoon salt
2 tablespoons soy sauce
2 tablespoons ketchup
3 tablespoons cornstarch,
  dissolved in 1 cup cold
  water
1/4 cup white vinegar
1/2 cup sugar

Mix all the ingredients in a small pot and simmer over low heat for 3 minutes, stirring constantly until the mixture thickens. Cool and serve with meat, fish or Fried Shrimp Wontons (see page 28).

*Makes 1 1/2 cups.*

# VINEGAR SAUCE

1 fresh cayenne pepper,
  minced
1/4 cup rice vinegar
1/4 cup soy sauce
1/2 teaspoon sugar

Combine all the ingredients in a small bowl. Stir well and refrigerate before serving. Serve with meat, fish or shrimp.

*Makes 1/2 cup.*

# CHAPTER TWO

# APPETIZERS

# &

# SNACKS

# CHAPTER TWO

## Appetizers and Snacks

# BARBECUED PORK

2 lbs. boneless pork shoulder
   or butt, excess fat trimmed
3 tablespoons rice wine
2 thin slices fresh ginger
3 cloves garlic, crushed
1 teaspoon five-spice powder
1/4 cup light soy sauce
1/4 cup brown sugar
1/4 cup hoisin sauce
1/4 cup ketchup
1 tablespoon honey
2 green onions, cut into
   1-inch lengths
2 cups cold water

Cut the pork into 2 inch wide and 6 inch long strips. Marinate the pork with the wine, ginger, garlic, five-spice powder, soy sauce, sugar, hoisin sauce, ketchup, honey, and green onions for 2 hours or overnight, refrigerated. Place the pork strips on the rack of a 9X13 inch baking pan lined with aluminum foil. Reserve the remaining marinade for basting. Add the cold water to the bottom of the pan. Preheat the oven to 425 degrees and bake the pork strips for 15 minutes, basting occasionally with the reserved marinade. Reduce the heat to 350 degrees and bake for 20 minutes. Turn the pork strips, baste the other side, and bake for 15 minutes. Broil the pork strips on each side for 2 minutes or until light golden brown. Cool before cutting. Slice the pork strips diagonally into 1/4 inch-thick pieces. Serve warm or cold with Hot Mustard Sauce (see page 17).

*Serves 4-6.*

# CHICKEN SPRING ROLLS

**2 lbs. chicken breast, boned, skinned, and shredded**
**1 teaspoon salt**
**2 tablespoons cornstarch**
**3 tablespoons canola oil**
**1 onion, minced**
**3 cloves garlic, minced**
**1 large carrot, peeled, cut into julienne strips**
**1/2 cup bamboo shoots, shredded**
**1 pkg. spring roll wrappers (25 square wrappers)**
**1 egg white**
**2 cups canola oil for deep-frying**

In a small bowl, mix the chicken, salt, and cornstarch. Set aside. Heat the oil in a large wok and sauté the onion and garlic until golden brown. Add the marinated chicken and sauté for 3 minutes. Add the carrot and bamboo shoots and sauté for 2 minutes, stirring frequently. Turn off the heat and pour the mixture into a colander. Drain the liquid and let it cool before wrapping. Place a wrapper with one corner toward you. On each corner, brush on a little of the egg white to seal the edges of the spring roll. Put two tablespoons of the mixture 1/3 of the way from the closest edge. Fold the closest edge over the filling, then fold over the right and left edges, then roll it up very tightly (see diagram, page 146). Continue making the spring rolls until all are ready. Place the finished rolls, seam side down, on a large flat serving platter until ready to fry. Heat the oil in a large wok and carefully place 3 rolls at a time in the hot oil and deep-fry them slowly until both sides are golden brown, about 2 minutes each side. Remove and drain on paper towels. Serve with Sweet and Sour Sauce (see page 20). Serve hot.

*Serves 6-8.*

# CHINESE PANCAKES

**2 cups flour**
**2/3 cup boiling water**
**2 teaspoons canola oil**

In a large bowl, stir together the flour, boiling water, and oil until a dough forms. Knead the dough on a lightly floured surface for 5 minutes or until smooth. Cover the dough with a damp dish towel and let it stand for 30 minutes. Divide the dough into 12 pieces and roll each piece into a 6-inch round. Cook each pancake over low heat in a preheated nonstick frying pan until light brown spots appear underneath. Serve warm with Mu Shu Pork (see page 124), or Crispy Roast Duck (see page 122).

*Makes 10.*

# CURRIED PORK TURNOVERS

2 tablespoons canola oil
1 small onion, finely chopped
3 cloves garlic, minced
1 lb. ground pork (Beef,
   shrimp, or chicken may
   also be used.)
1 teaspoon salt
1 teaspoon ground white
   pepper
1 teaspoon sugar
1 tablespoon curry powder
3 cups flour, sifted
2/3 cup butter or margarine
3 tablespoons cold water
4 egg yolks

Heat the oil in a wok and sauté the onion and garlic until golden brown. Add the pork, salt, pepper, sugar, and curry powder and sauté for 3 minutes or until the pork is cooked. Remove and set it aside until it cools. Make the dough in a large bowl by thoroughly mixing the flour, butter, cold water, and 2 of the egg yolks. Roll out the dough into circles 4 inches in diameter and 1/8 inch thick. Put 1 tablespoon of the filling halfway from the edge. Fold the bare side over the filling. Crimp the edges together with a fork. Brush each one with the remaining 2 beaten egg yolks. Bake in a 375 degree oven for 20 minutes or until the top of the dough is light golden brown.

*Serves 6-8.*

# DEEP-FRIED CHICKEN WINGS

2 lbs. chicken wings
1/2 teaspoon salt
1 tablespoon soy sauce
2 tablespoons rice wine
3 cloves garlic, minced
1/2 teaspoon ground white
  pepper
1/2 teaspoon five-spice
  powder
1 egg white, beaten
1/2 cup cornstarch
2 cups canola oil for
  deep-frying

In a large bowl, marinate the chicken wings with the salt, soy sauce, wine, garlic, pepper, five-spice powder, and egg white for at least 20 minutes or overnight, refrigerated. Coat each marinated chicken wing with cornstarch on both sides. Heat the oil in a large wok over medium heat and deep-fry for 3 minutes on each side or until the chicken wings are golden brown and completely cooked throughout. Serve with Sweet and Sour Sauce (see page 20).

*Serves 4-6.*

# FRIED SHRIMP WONTONS

2 lbs. shrimp, shelled and deveined (see diagram, page 145), finely chopped
1 egg, beaten
4 green onions, minced
3 cloves garlic, minced
1/2 teaspoon salt
1/2 teaspoon ground white pepper
6 whole water chestnuts, minced
1 tablespoon cornstarch
1 teaspoon sesame oil
1 pkg. wonton wrappers
2 cups canola oil for deep-frying

In a small bowl, thoroughly mix the shrimp, egg white, green onions, garlic, salt, pepper, water chestnuts, cornstarch, and sesame oil. Place 1 teaspoon of the shrimp mixture in the center of each wonton wrapper. Wet the edges of the wrapper and fold it up, corner to corner, pinching together the 3 corners so that the filled wonton folds up into a triangle. Next, wet one of the bottom corners of the triangle and fold it over to join with the opposite corner with both sides overlapping. Then pinch them together (see diagram, 144). (Another method of filling the wonton wrappers is to wet the four corners and bunch them together to form a flower.) Heat the oil in a wok and deep-fry the wontons for about 2 minutes on each side or until light golden brown. Serve with Sweet and Sour Sauce (see page 20).

*Serves 4-6.*

# HARD-BOILED TEA EGGS

**10 cups water**
**12 eggs**
**1 teaspoon salt**
**1 tablespoon five-spice**
  **powder**
**3 tablespoons soy sauce**
**8 teabags or 6 tablespoons**
  **black tea**
**3 star anise**
**1 small piece of cinnamon**
  **stick**

In a large deep pot, bring the water, eggs, salt, five-spice powder, soy sauce, tea, anise, and cinnamon stick to a boil. Reduce the heat to low and simmer for about 30 minutes. Remove the eggs and let them cool. Reserve the water. Tap the shells very lightly all over to form hairline cracks. Try not to break through the shell. Do not remove the shells. Put the eggs back into the reserved water and refrigerate overnight. Remove the eggs from the water and refrigerate. Peel the egg shells just before serving. The peeled eggs have a beautifully marbled appearance and delicious spicy flavor. (Tea eggs are very good to use for eggs in Easter egg hunts.)

*Serves 8-10.*

# Pearl Balls

**1 1/2 lbs. ground pork**
**1/4 cup dried shrimp, soaked in 1/2 cup of warm water for 5 minutes, drained and minced**
**1 large egg**
**2 green onions, finely chopped**
**1 teaspoon ginger, finely chopped**
**1 teaspoon salt**
**3 tablespoons cornstarch**
**2 cups white glutinous rice, soaked in cold water for about 1 hour, drained**

In a large bowl, thoroughly mix the pork, minced shrimp, egg, green onions, ginger, salt, and 1 tablespoon of cornstarch. Set the mixture aside. Sprinkle the 2 remaining tablespoons of cornstarch on a tray, then layer the glutinous rice on top of the cornstarch. Now shape the mixture into 2-inch balls and roll and rock them back and forth on the tray so that the glutinous rice sticks to all sides of the meat balls. Again put the meat balls in your palm and shape them until they are round. Place the Pearl Balls in a steamer on a damp cloth and steam them for about 20 to 25 minutes over high heat. Remove and place them on a large platter. Serve hot.

*Makes 35 to 40.*

# PICKLED BROCCOLI STALKS

1 1/2 lbs. broccoli stalks,
  woody ends and hard
  skin removed
2 tablespoons sesame oil
1/4 cup light soy sauce
3 cloves garlic, minced
1 fresh red cayenne pepper,
  sliced

Cut the broccoli stalks into 2-inch lengths and then cut them into thin slices. In a small bowl, thoroughly mix the sliced broccoli stalks, sesame oil, soy sauce, garlic, and cayenne pepper. Marinate at least 30 minutes in the refrigerator before serving.

*Serves 4-6.*

# POTSTICKERS

1 lb. ground pork
2 bunches Chinese chives,
  finely chopped
4 cloves garlic, finely
  chopped
1 teaspoon salt
1 teaspoon ground white
  pepper
2 teaspoons sesame oil
1 pkg. Potsticker Wrappers
1 tablespoon canola oil for
  each batch of potstickers
water for cooking

In a large bowl, thoroughly mix the pork, Chinese chives, garlic, salt, white pepper, and sesame oil. Place one teaspoonful of the pork mixture in the center of a wrapper. Wet all around the edges of the wrapper, then fold it over to make a half circle and crimp the edges together to seal. Heat the oil in a large frying pan and place enough dumplings to cover the bottom of the frying pan without overlapping. Fry the dumplings over a medium high heat for a few seconds until the bottom is light golden brown. Lower the heat and add 1/2 of a cup of water and cover. Cook until the water has evaporated. Repeat the process until all the Potsticker Wrappers are used. Serve hot with Garlic Sauce (see page 15).

*Serves 4-6.*

# Shao Mai

4 dried black Chinese mushrooms, soaked in 1/4 cup of warm water for 15 minutes (discard the water), finely chopped (Note: Discard the hard ends from the stems.)

2 lbs. ground pork

1/2 cup canned bamboo shoots, finely chopped

1 teaspoon salt

1/2 teaspoon ground white pepper

1 tablespoon cornstarch

1 egg, beaten

3 cloves garlic, minced

1 teaspoon sesame oil

1 pkg. Shao Mai or wonton wrappers

In a large bowl, mix thoroughly the black Chinese mushrooms, pork, bamboo shoots, salt, pepper, cornstarch, egg, garlic, and sesame oil. Divide the pork mixture into 40 equal portions. Place 1 portion in the center of each wrapper. Pleat the wrapper around the filling to make a little pouch, leaving the top open. Dip a teaspoon in cold water and smooth the filling on top. Arrange as many Shao Mai on a damp cloth in a large steamer as will fit without touching each other. Cover the steamer and steam over high heat for 10 minutes. Serve with Vinegar Sauce (see page 20) or Ginger Sauce (see page 15).

*Makes 35 to 40.*

# SPICY SHRIMP BALLS

2 lbs. large shrimp, shelled, deveined (see diagram, page 145)
1/2 teaspoon salt
1 teaspoon sugar
1/2 teaspoon ground white pepper
1/2 cup canned water chestnuts, minced
1/4 cup tapioca flour
2 egg whites
2 fresh red cayenne peppers, minced
4 green onions, minced
1 tablespoon rice wine
1 tablespoon oyster sauce
1 teaspoon sesame oil
2 cups canola oil for deep-frying
2 tablespoons canola oil for oiling the spoon and palm of your hand

In a blender, blend the shrimp into a smooth paste. In a large bowl, thoroughly mix the ground shrimp, salt, sugar, pepper, water chestnuts, tapioca flour, egg whites, cayenne peppers, green onions, rice wine, oyster sauce, and sesame oil. Put a little oil on the palm of one hand and place 3 tablespoons of the shrimp mixture in it. Close your hand into a fist and squeeze out an amount about the size of a walnut from the top. Then take an oiled spoon, remove the squeezed out ball and place it on an oiled cookie sheet. Continue squeezing out the shrimp balls in the same way until all the mixture is used. Heat the oil in a large wok and deep-fry the shrimp balls for 3 minutes on each side or until golden brown on both sides. Remove and drain on paper towels. Serve with Ginger Sauce (see page 15), or Sweet and Sour Sauce (see page 20).

*Serves 4-6.*

# STEAMED SPARERIBS

2 lbs. pork spareribs, cut into
  1-inch pieces (For ease,
  ask the butcher to cut
  the spareribs.)
2 tablespoons light soy sauce
1 tablespoon rice wine
3 green onions, minced
4 cloves garlic, minced
2 tablespoons salted black
  beans (Chinese style),
  minced
1 teaspoon Chinese five-spice
  powder
1/8 teaspoon salt
1/2 teaspoon sugar
1/4 cup cornstarch

In a large bowl, marinate the ribs with soy sauce, rice wine, green onions, garlic, salted black beans, five-spice powder, salt, and sugar for 1 hour or overnight in a refrigerator. Coat the ribs with the cornstarch and place them onto an oiled 9-inch heatproof plate. Put the plate of ribs in the steamer and pour any remaining marinade over the ribs. Cover and steam for 45 minutes or until the ribs are tender.

*Serves 4-6.*

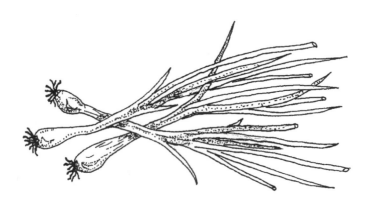

# CHAPTER THREE

# SOUPS

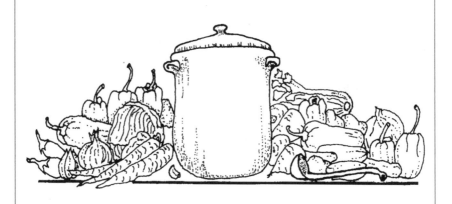

# CHAPTER THREE

## Soups

# ABALONE SOUP

8 cups water

4 dried black Chinese mushrooms, soaked in 1/4 cup of warm water for 15 minutes (reserve the water), thinly sliced (Note: Discard the hard ends from the stems.)

1 lb. chicken thighs, skinned

3 thin slices fresh ginger

1 tablespoon rice wine

1 teaspoon salt

1/2 teaspoon ground white pepper

1 can abalone (4 oz.), drained (reserve the water), thinly sliced

2 teaspoons sesame oil

3 green onions, chopped

Bring the water to a boil in a large pot. Add the Chinese mushrooms, reserved mushroom soaking water, chicken, ginger, rice wine, salt, and pepper and simmer for 40 minutes or until the chicken thighs are cooked. Add the abalone with the water and simmer for 1 minute. Drizzle with the sesame oil and garnish with the green onions.

*Serves 4-6.*

# CHICKEN AND ASPARAGUS SOUP

8 cups chicken broth
1/2 lb. fresh green asparagus, cleaned, and cut into 2-inch lengths
3 tablespoons light soy sauce
1 teaspoon sugar
1/2 cup cellophane noodles, soaked in warm water for 5 minutes, drained, cut into 4-inch lengths
2 thin slices fresh ginger
1 cup cooked chicken breast, skinned, shredded
1/2 teaspoon white pepper
1/4 teaspoon salt
4 green onions, finely chopped

Bring the chicken broth to a boil in a large deep pot. Add the asparagus, soy sauce, and sugar and simmer for 3 minutes. Add the cellophane noodles, ginger, chicken, pepper, and salt. Simmer for 2 more minutes. Garnish with the green onions.

*Serves 6-8.*

# CHICKEN AND CREAMED CORN SOUP

2 tablespoons canola oil

1 yellow onion, finely chopped

3 cloves garlic, minced

2 quarts chicken broth

2 cans creamed corn (17 oz. each)

1 teaspoon salt

1 teaspoon ground white pepper

1 whole chicken breast, boned, skinned, thinly sliced

3 tablespoons cornstarch, dissolved in 1/4 cup of cold water

2 eggs, well beaten

1 teaspoon sesame oil

2 green onions, finely chopped

1/4 cup fresh coriander leaves, chopped

Heat the oil in a large pot and sauté the onion and garlic until light golden brown. Add the chicken broth and creamed corn. Bring to a boil and add the salt, pepper, and chicken. Reduce the heat to low and simmer for 3 minutes. Stir the cornstarch mixture into the soup until it thickens slightly. Stir well and gradually add in the beaten eggs. Reduce the heat to low and simmer for a few seconds. Drizzle with the sesame oil and garnish with the green onions and coriander leaves.

*Serves 6-8.*

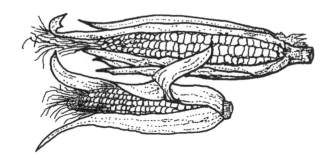

# CHICKEN CONGEE

1 cup white short grain rice, washed, drained

10 cups chicken broth

1 one-inch piece fresh ginger, cut into julienne strips

2 lbs. boneless chicken breast, skinned, thinly sliced

1/2 teaspoon ground white pepper

1 teaspoon salt

3 tablespoons canola oil

3 cloves garlic, minced

4 green onions, finely chopped

1/4 cup celery leaves, finely chopped

1/4 cup fresh coriander leaves, chopped

1/4 cup peanuts, roasted, crushed

In a large uncovered pot, bring the rice, chicken broth, and ginger to a boil. Reduce the heat to low and simmer for about 40 minutes or until the rice is soft. Set the pot aside. Season the chicken slices with pepper and salt and refrigerate for 5 minutes. Heat the oil in a large wok and stir-fry the garlic and seasoned chicken for 2 minutes, stirring frequently. Lower the heat and simmer for 3 minutes or until the chicken pieces are cooked. In small bowls, put 1 cup of the heated rice broth along with some chicken. Garnish with the green onions, celery leaves, coriander leaves, and crushed peanuts.

*Serves 8.*

# CREAMY CRAB CORN SOUP

6 cups chicken broth
1 lb. boneless chicken breast, skinned, thinly sliced
1 can creamed corn (17 oz.)
1 cup canned crab meat
3 tablespoons cornstarch, dissolved in 1/4 cup of cold water
1/2 teaspoon ground white pepper
1/2 teaspoon salt
4 green onions, finely chopped
1/4 cup fresh coriander leaves, chopped

Bring the chicken broth to a boil in a large pot. Add the sliced chicken, creamed corn, and crab meat, and bring it to a boil for about 10 minutes. Pour the cornstarch mixture, pepper, and salt into the soup and stir well. Simmer for 5 minutes and garnish with the green onions and coriander leaves. Serve hot.

*Serves 4-6.*

# CUCUMBER WITH PORK SOUP

1/2 lb. pork loin, thinly sliced
2 tablespoons light soy sauce
2 tablespoons cornstarch
8 cups chicken broth
2 cucumbers, peeled, seeded, cut in half lengthwise and sliced crosswise into 1-inch pieces
1/2 teaspoon salt
1/2 teaspoon ground white pepper
2 teaspoons sesame oil
3 tablespoons fresh coriander leaves, chopped

In a small bowl, mix the pork, soy sauce, and cornstarch. Place the mixture in the refrigerator for 5 minutes. Bring the chicken broth to a boil in a large pot. Add the pork and cook for 10 minutes. Add the cucumber, salt, and pepper. Cover and cook for 3 minutes. Drizzle with the sesame oil and garnish with the coriander leaves.

*Serves 4-6.*

# HOT AND SOUR SOUP

8 cups chicken broth
1 large carrot, peeled, cut into julienne strips
1/4 lb. tenderloin pork, thinly sliced
1 cup canned bamboo shoots in strips
1 tablespoon chili sauce or 4 fresh red cayenne peppers, minced
1/4 cup white vinegar
1/2 teaspoon salt
2 tablespoons soy sauce
2 tablespoons sugar
6 dried black Chinese mushrooms, soaked in 1/4 cup of warm water for 10 minutes (reserve the water), cut into julienne strips (Note: Discard the hard ends from the stems.)
1/4 cup cornstarch, dissolved in 1/2 cup of cold water
2 eggs, well beaten
1 cup firm tofu, cut into julienne strips
1 tablespoon sesame oil
4 green onions, chopped
1/4 cup fresh coriander leaves, chopped

Bring the chicken broth to a boil in a large deep pot. Add the carrot, pork, bamboo shoots, chili sauce, vinegar, salt, soy sauce, sugar, Chinese mushrooms, and reserved mushroom soaking water. Reduce the heat to low and simmer for 10 minutes. Stir the cornstarch mixture into the soup until it thickens slightly. Stir well and gradually add in the beaten eggs and tofu. Reduce the heat to low and simmer for 1 minute. Drizzle with the sesame oil and garnish with the green onions and coriander leaves.

*Serves 6-8.*

# Mushroom Soup

**6 cups chicken broth or water**
**1/2 lb. boneless chicken breast, skinned, thinly sliced, coated with 2 tablespoons cornstarch**
**1/2 lb. fresh mushrooms, washed, thinly sliced**
**3 tablespoons cornstarch, dissolved in 1/4 cup of cold water**
**4 egg whites, beaten**
**1/2 teaspoon salt**
**1/2 teaspoon ground white pepper**
**4 green onions, finely chopped**
**1 teaspoon sesame oil**

In a large pot, bring the chicken broth to a boil. Add the coated chicken slices and return to a boil for 5 minutes. Add the mushrooms and cornstarch mixture into the soup until it thickens slightly. Stir well and gradually add in the beaten egg whites, stirring constantly. Simmer for 1 minute and add the salt, pepper, and green onions. Drizzle with the sesame oil.

*Serves 4-6.*

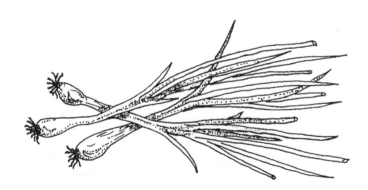

# MUSTARD GREEN SOUP

1/4 lb. tenderloin pork, thinly
  sliced
1 tablespoon light soy sauce
1/4 teaspoon ground white
  pepper
1 tablespoon cornstarch
6 cups chicken broth or water
1/4 lb. fresh mustard greens,
  washed, cut into 2-inch
  lengths
1/4 teaspoon salt
2 green onions, chopped
1 teaspoon sesame oil

In a small bowl, mix the pork, soy sauce, pepper, and cornstarch. Set aside for 5 minutes in the refrigerator. Bring the chicken broth to a boil in a large pot. Add the pork mixture and cook for 3 minutes. Add the mustard greens and salt and simmer for 1 minute. Do not overcook. Garnish with the green onions and drizzle with the sesame oil.

*Serves 4-6.*

# OXTAIL SOUP

2 tablespoons canola oil
1 large yellow onion, chopped
8 cloves garlic, crushed
1 teaspoon minced fresh
  ginger
8 star anise
5 quarts of water
3 lbs. oxtail, excess fat
  removed
3 large potatoes, peeled, cut
  into 2-inch lengths
3 large carrots, peeled, cut
  into 1-inch lengths
4 green onions, chopped
1/4 cup fresh coriander
  leaves, chopped

In a large deep pot with oil, sauté the onion, garlic, ginger, and star anise until light golden brown. Add the water and bring to a boil. Add the oxtail and bring to a boil, then reduce the heat to low and simmer for 3 1/2 hours or until the meat is tender. Add the potatoes and carrots and simmer for 30 minutes. Skim off the excess fat from the top of the soup and garnish with the green onions, coriander leaves, and Aromatic Fried Shallots (see page 13) just before serving.

*Serves 6-8.*

# SPINACH SOUP WITH SOY BEAN PASTE

5 cups water
1 pkg. firm tofu (16 oz.),
   drained, cubed
2 tablespoons soy bean
   paste (Miso)
1 lb. fresh spinach, cleaned,
   drained, cut into 2-inch
   lengths
4 green onions, finely
   chopped
2 teaspoons sesame oil

Bring the water to a boil in a large pot. Reduce the heat to low and add the tofu and soy bean paste and simmer for 3 minutes. Stir in the spinach, green onions, and sesame oil and simmer for a few seconds. Do not overcook the spinach. Serve immediately.

*Serves 4-6.*


# SPINACH TOFU SOUP

2 tablespoons canola oil
1 small onion, finely chopped
3 cloves garlic, minced
6 cups beef broth or water
1 teaspoon salt
1 pkg. firm tofu (16 oz.),
   drained, cubed
1 lb. spinach, washed,
   drained, cut into 2-inch
   lengths
1 teaspoon sesame oil

Heat the oil in a large pot and sauté the onion and garlic until light golden brown. Add the beef broth, salt, and tofu and bring the soup to a boil. Add the spinach and stir with a wooden spoon for a few seconds and turn off the stove. Do not overcook the spinach. Drizzle with the sesame oil.

*Serves 4-6.*

# Tomato and Tofu Soup

1 tablespoon canola oil
3 cloves garlic, minced
2 large tomatoes, cubed
1 teaspoon salt
6 cups chicken broth or water
1 pkg. firm tofu (16 oz.),
　drained, cubed
1/2 teaspoon ground white
　pepper
2 tablespoons cornstarch,
　dissolved in 1/4 cup of
　cold water
2 eggs, beaten
2 green onions, chopped
1 teaspoon sesame oil

Heat the oil in a large deep pot and sauté the garlic until light brown. Add the tomatoes, salt, chicken broth, tofu, and pepper and bring to a boil for 5 minutes. Add the cornstarch mixture and stir well. Slowly pour the eggs onto the surface of the soup while stirring gently in a circular pattern to form thin threads of cooked egg. Reduce the heat to low and simmer for 1 minute. Garnish with the green onions and drizzle with the sesame oil.

*Serves 4-6.*

# Watercress Soup with Pork

1/2 lb. pork loin, thinly sliced
1/2 teaspoon ground white
　pepper
1 egg white
3 tablespoons cornstarch
8 cups chicken broth or water
1 teaspoon salt
1 bunch watercress, washed,
　drained, cut into 2-inch
　lengths

In a small bowl, mix the pork, pepper, eggwhite, and conrstarch. Set aside for 5 minutes in the refrigerator. In a large pot, bring the chicken broth to a boil. Add the salt and pork mixture and cook for 5 minutes. Add the watercress and stir for a few seconds. Do not overcook the watercress by waiting for the soup to come to a boil again. Serve immediately.

*Serves 6-8.*

# White Icicle Radish Soup

6 cups water
1/2 lb. top sirloin beef, thinly sliced, coated with 2 tablespoons of cornstarch
1/2 teaspoon salt
3 tablespoons light soy sauce
1 large white icicle radish (daikon), peeled, cut into 1-inch cubes
1 one-inch piece fresh ginger, thinly sliced
1/2 teaspoon ground white pepper
1/4 cup celery leaves, finely chopped

Bring the water to a boil in a large deep pot. Add the coated beef slices, salt, soy sauce, icicle radish, ginger, and pepper and bring it back to a boil. Reduce the heat to low and simmer for 20 minutes or until the beef and icicle radish are tender. Garnish with the celery leaves.

*Serves 4-6.*

# Wintermelon Soup

8 cups chicken broth or water
1/4 lb. tenderloin pork, thinly sliced
2 lbs. wintermelon, peeled, seeded, cut into 2-inch cubes
1 teaspoon salt
1/2 teaspoon ground black pepper
8 dried black fungus, soaked in warm water for 10 minutes, washed, drained, hard ends discarded from the fungus, cut in half
4 green onions, minced

In a large deep pot, bring the chicken broth to a boil. Add the pork and wintermelon and bring it to a boil for 2 minutes. Lower the heat and add the salt and pepper. Simmer for 20 minutes. Add the black fungus and cook for 5 minutes. Garnish with the green onions.

*Serves 8-10.*

# WONTON SOUP

**1/2 lb. lean ground pork**
**1/4 lb. shrimp, shelled**
   **(see diagram, page 145),**
   **minced**
**1 egg, beaten**
**2 green onions, minced**
**1 teaspoon salt**
**1 tablespoon sesame oil**
**1 tablespoon cornstarch**
**1 pkg. wonton wrappers**
**6 cups chicken broth**
**2 quarts water**
**4 green onions, chopped**

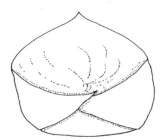

In a small bowl, thoroughly mix the pork, shrimp, egg, minced green onions, salt, sesame oil, and cornstarch. Place 1 teaspoon of the pork mixture in the center or each wonton wrapper. Wet the edges of the wrapper and fold it up, corner to corner, pinching together the 3 corners so that the filled wonton folds up into a triangle. Next, wet one of the bottom corners of the triangle and fold it over to join with the opposite corner with both sides overlapping. Then pinch them together (see diagram, page 144). (Another method of filling the wonton wrappers is to wet the four corners and bunch them together to form a flower.) In a large pot, bring the chicken broth to a boil and set it aside. In a deep pot, bring the water to a boil and drop the wontons into the boiling water, uncovered, for 3 minutes. When the water boils again, add 1 cup of cold water, then bring it back to a boil for 1 minute. Remove the wontons with a slotted spoon. In small bowls, put 1 cup of the heated chicken broth and add 5 cooked wontons to each bowl. Garnish with the green onions.

*Serves 4-6.*

# CHAPTER FOUR

# SALADS

# Salads

# ALMOND CHICKEN SALAD

4 cups water
2 lbs. boneless chicken
　breasts, skinned
2 stalks celery, thinly sliced
1/4 cup sesame seeds,
　roasted
1/2 cup slivered almonds,
　toasted
4 green onions, finely
　chopped
1/2 cup fresh coriander
　leaves, chopped
1/4 cup rice vinegar
2 teaspoons sesame oil
2 teaspoons brown sugar
1 teaspoon salt
1/2 teaspoon ground white
　pepper
2 tablespoons canola oil

Bring the water to a boil in a large pot and put the chicken breasts into the boiling water and cook for 40 minutes or until the chicken is done. Remove and cut into cubes. In a large salad bowl, arrange the chicken, celery, sesame seeds, slivered almonds, green onions, and coriander leaves in layers. In a small bowl, mix the vinegar, sesame oil, sugar, salt, pepper, and oil. Pour the dressing over the salad and toss.

*Serves 4-6.*

# ASPARAGUS SALAD

3 cups water
2 lbs. fresh asparagus,
   washed, hard ends trimmed
1/2 cup walnuts, roasted,
   finely chopped
2 teaspoons sesame oil
2 tablespoons rice vinegar
2 tablespoons light soy sauce
1 teaspoon sugar
4 green onions, finely
   chopped

Bring the water to a boil in a large pot. Add the asparagus and boil for 3 minutes or until just tender. Do not overcook. Place the asparagus in a large bowl. Set aside. In a small deep bowl, combine the walnuts, sesame oil, rice vinegar, soy sauce, sugar, and green onions. Pour the dressing over the asparagus and toss well. Refrigerate before serving.

*Serves 4-6.*

# BEAN SPROUT SALAD

2 cups water
2 lbs. bean sprouts, root
  ends trimmed
1 tablespoon canola oil
6 green onions, chopped
1/4 cup rice vinegar
1/2 teaspoon salt
1 teaspoon sugar
1 fresh red cayenne pepper,
  sliced
2 teaspoons sesame oil
1/4 cup fresh coriander
  leaves, chopped

Bring the water to a boil in a large pot. Drop the bean sprouts in and remove them after 5 seconds. Do not overcook. Place the bean sprouts in a colander and rinse under cold water. The sprouts should still be crunchy. Drain the bean sprouts for 5 minutes or until all water is gone. Place them in a large salad bowl. Heat the oil in a small pot and stir-fry the green onions for a few seconds. Remove from the heat and add the vinegar, salt, sugar, cayenne pepper, and oil and stir until well blended. Pour the dressing over the bean sprouts and mix well. Garnish with the coriander leaves. Refrigerate the bean sprout salad before serving.

*Serves 4-6.*

# CAULIFLOWER SALAD

2 quarts water
2 lbs. cauliflower, washed,
   cut into small florets
1 teaspoon minced ginger
3 cloves garlic, minced
4 green onions, (white part
   only) minced
1/4 cup sugar
1 teaspoon salt
juice of 1 lime
1/4 cup white vinegar
2 fresh red cayenne peppers,
   sliced

Bring the water to a boil in a large pot. Add the cauliflower florets and boil for 5 minutes. Remove them from the heat and drain them. Place the cauliflower florets in a large salad bowl and add the ginger, garlic, green onions, sugar, salt, lime juice, vinegar, and cayenne peppers and mix until well blended. Refrigerate for at least 4 hours or overnight before serving.

*Serves 4-6.*

# CELERY SALAD

6 stalks celery, cut into
   2-inch julienne strips
1 teaspoon salt
1 teaspoon sugar
1/4 cup rice vinegar
1 fresh red cayenne
   pepper, sliced
1 teaspoon sesame oil

Place the celery in a large bowl. Stir in the salt, sugar, vinegar, cayenne pepper, and sesame oil. Refrigerate until ready to serve.

*Serves 4-6.*

# CHICKEN SALAD WITH MUSTARD

2 cups cooked chicken
  breast, skinned, shredded
2 ripe tomatoes, cubed
1 cucumber, peeled, seeded,
  cubed
2 tablespoons Dijon mustard
1/4 cup sesame oil
2 tablespoons rice vinegar
1 teaspoon salt
2 green onions, chopped
1/4 cup fresh coriander
  leaves, chopped
1 tablespoon sesame seeds,
  toasted

In a large salad bowl, arrange the chicken, tomatoes and cucumber in layers. In a small bowl, mix the mustard, sesame oil, vinegar, and salt. Pour the dressing over the salad and toss. Garnish with the green onions and coriander leaves. Sprinkle with the sesame seeds.

*Serves 4-6.*

# EGGPLANT SALAD

8 small Japanese eggplants
2 tablespoons canola oil
6 cloves garlic, minced
4 green onions, finely
  chopped
2 fresh red cayenne peppers,
  minced
3 tablespoons light soy sauce
2 teaspoons brown sugar
2 teaspoons sesame oil
1/4 cup fresh coriander leaves

Slice the eggplant crosswise on a diagonal into 1/8-inch thick slices. Heat the oil in a large wok and sauté the garlic, green onions, and cayenne peppers for a few seconds. Add the eggplant and stir-fry for 3 minutes, stirring frequently. Add the soy sauce and sugar. Bring to a simmer, cover, and cook for 5 minutes or until the eggplant is tender. Do not overcook. Drizzle with the sesame oil. Let the salad cool and refrigerate before serving. Garnish with the coriander leaves.

*Serves 4-6.*

# Garlic Cucumber Salad

2 lbs. fresh pickling
  cucumbers
1 teaspoon salt
2 tablespoons sugar
4 cloves garlic, minced
3 tablespoons light soy sauce
2 tablespoons white vinegar
1 teaspoon sesame oil

Lightly crush the cucumbers with the broad side of a cleaver to release their flavor. Cut them diagonally into 1-inch slices. In a small bowl, rub the cucumber pieces with salt. Let them stand for 20 minutes. Rinse them with cold water and drain well. Add the sugar, garlic, soy sauce, vinegar, and sesame oil. Cover and refrigerate for at least 4 hours before serving. The garlic cucumber salad will keep in the refrigerator up to one week.

*Serves 4-6.*

# Jicama Salad

2 lbs. jicama, peeled, cut
  into 2-inch julienne strips
1 teaspoon salt
1/4 cup fresh lime juice or
  white vinegar
2 tablespoons sugar

In a large salad bowl, mix thoroughly the jicama, salt, lime juice, and sugar until well blended. Refrigerate for at least 4 hours or overnight before serving. The jicama salad will keep in the refrigerator up to one week.

*Serves 4-6.*

# Lotus Salad

1 lb. lotus root, peeled
2 cups water
1 tablespoon canola oil
2 green onions, minced
2 tablespoons rice vinegar
1 tablespoon sugar
1/2 teaspoon salt
1 red cayenne pepper, sliced

Cut the lotus root crosswise into 1/4-inch thick slices. Bring the water to a boil in a large pot. Add the lotus and boil for 10 minutes. Drain and rinse in cold water. Place in a large serving bowl. Heat the oil in a small pot and sauté the green onions for a few seconds. Remove from the heat and add the vinegar, sugar, salt and cayenne pepper and stir until well blended. Pour the dressing over the lotus and serve immediately.

*Serves 4-6.*

# Pickled Szechwan Salad

1/2 lb. green cabbage, cored, cut into 1-inch cubes
2 large carrots, peeled, cut diagonally into 1/8-inch slices
3 small cucumbers, peeled, cut diagonally into 1/8-inch slices
6 red cayenne peppers, sliced
1 one-inch piece fresh ginger, sliced
1 tablespoon Szechwan peppercorns
1 tablespoon salt
1/2 cup sugar
1 cup rice vinegar
1 quart cold water

Combine all the ingredients in a large bowl. Pour the mixture into a large jar or crock. Cover tightly and refrigerate for 3 days. Drain the liquid before serving. Serve as an appetizer or as a salad. If you do not want to eat all the salad in one serving, you can store it covered in the refrigerator with the liquid for up to 2 weeks.

*Serves 4-6.*

# SHRIMP AND SNOW PEA SALAD

2 cups water
1 lb. snow peas, ends
removed, washed
1 lb. shrimp, shelled,
deveined (see diagram,
page 145), cooked
1 can water chestnuts (4 oz.),
drained, sliced
2 tablespoons sesame oil
3 tablespoons light soy sauce
1 tablespoon white rice
vinegar
1 teaspoon brown sugar
1/2 teaspoon ground white
pepper
4 green onions, finely
chopped
3 tablespoons toasted
sesame seeds

Bring the water to a boil in a large pot. Add the snow peas and cook for a few seconds or until just softened. Do not overcook. Drain and rinse under cold water. Drain and cool. In a large bowl, arrange the snow peas, shrimp, and water chestnuts. In a small bowl, mix the sesame oil, soy sauce, vinegar, sugar, and pepper. Pour the dressing over the salad and toss. Garnish with the green onions and sprinkle with the sesame seeds.

*Serves 6-8.*

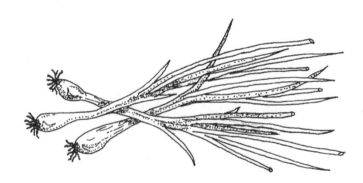

# Spicy Chinese Cabbage Salad

2 lbs. Chinese cabbage, cut
 into 2-inch lengths
1 tablespoon salt
4 cloves garlic, minced
1/4 cup sugar
8 dried hot red cayenne
 peppers, sliced
1/2 cup rice vinegar

In a large bowl, rub the cabbage with salt. Let stand for 2 hours. Place the cabbage in a colander and rinse with cold water. Drain the cabbage and squeeze to remove the water. Discard the water. Return the cabbage to the bowl, and add the garlic, sugar and peppers. In a small pot, bring the vinegar to a boil. Pour the vinegar over the cabbage mixture and mix well. Cool and refrigerate for 2 hours before serving.

*Serves 6-8.*

# Spicy Cucumber Salad

3 large cucumbers, peeled,
 cut in half lengthwise
1 teaspoon salt
1 tablespoon sugar
2 tablespoons white vinegar
2 fresh red cayenne peppers,
 sliced
2 teaspoons sesame oil
1/4 cup fresh coriander
 leaves

Slice the cucumbers into 1/2-inch slices. Place the cucumbers in a large salad bowl. Add the salt, sugar, vinegar, cayenne peppers, and sesame oil and mix until well blended. Garnish with the coriander leaves.

*Serves 4-6.*

# Spinach Salad

2 lbs. fresh spinach, washed, blanched
1 teaspoon chopped ginger
3 cloves garlic, minced
3 tablespoons light soy sauce
1 teaspoon sugar
1 teaspoon sesame oil
2 tablespoons fresh lime juice
1 fresh red cayenne pepper, sliced
2 green onions, finely chopped

Place the spinach in a large salad bowl. In a small bowl, combine the ginger, garlic, soy sauce, sugar, sesame oil, lime juice, cayenne pepper, and green onions. Pour the dressing over the spinach.

*Serves 4-6.*

# Szechwan Shrimp Salad

2 cups water
2 lbs. large shrimp, shelled, deveined (see diagram, page 145)
1 cucumber, peeled, cut into julienne strips
1 tablespoon roasted sesame seeds
1/4 cup fresh coriander leaves
1 teaspoon Szechwan peppercorns, roasted, ground
1/2 teaspoon salt
2 teaspoons sugar
juice of one lime
1 tablespoon chile oil

Bring the water to a boil in a large pot and cook the shrimp in the boiling water for 2 minutes or until tender. Do not overcook. Drain and cool. On a large deep serving platter, arrange the cooked shrimp, cucumber, sesame seeds, and coriander leaves. Set the platter aside. In a small bowl, thoroughly mix the peppercorns, salt, sugar, lime juice, and chile oil. Just before serving, pour the dressing over the salad.

*Serves 4-6.*

# CHAPTER FIVE

# VEGETABLES

# CHAPTER FIVE

## Vegetables

# ASPARAGUS WITH BABY CORN

2 tablespoons canola oil
4 cloves garlic, minced
1 large carrot, peeled,
  thinly sliced
1 lb. asparagus, cut into
  2-inch lengths, hard ends
  trimmed
1 cup canned baby corn,
  cut in half lengthwise
1 teaspoon salt

Heat the oil in a large wok and sauté the garlic for 5 seconds. Add the carrot, asparagus, baby corn, and salt and stir-fry for 2 minutes, stirring occasionally, or until the asparagus are crispy tender. Do not overcook.

*Serves 4-6.*

# ASPARAGUS WITH BLACK MUSHROOMS

2 tablespoons canola oil
3 cloves garlic, minced
6 dried black Chinese
  mushrooms, soaked in 1/4
  cup of warm water for 10
  minutes (reserve the water),
  cut in half (Note: Discard the
  hard ends from the stems.)
1/2 teaspoon salt
1 lb. asparagus, cut into
  2-inch lengths, hard ends
  trimmed
1 teaspoon cornstarch,
  dissolved in 1/4 cup of the
  reserved mushroom
  soaking water
2 tablespoons oyster sauce

Heat the oil in a large wok and stir-fry the garlic until light golden brown. Add the black mushrooms and salt and stir-fry for a few seconds. Add the asparagus and stir-fry for 1 minute, stirring frequently. Add the cornstarch mixture and oyster sauce and stir-fry until the sauce thickens.

*Serves 4-6.*

# BEAN CURD HOT POT

2 tablespoons canola oil

6 dried black Chinese
mushrooms, soaked in 1/2
cup of warm water for 10
minutes (reserve the water),
cut in half. (Note: Discard
the hard ends from the
stems.)

1/2 teaspoon salt

1 zucchini, sliced

1/2 cup canned, sliced
bamboo shoots

1/2 cup canned baby corn

1/2 cup canned sliced water
chestnuts

1 small leek (white part only),
shredded

1 pkg. fried tofu (10.5 oz.),
cubed

2 tablespoons light soy sauce

1 teaspoon sugar

1/2 teaspoon ground white
pepper

1 teaspoon sesame oil

2 teaspoons cornstarch,
dissolved in 1/4 cup of cold
water

6 outer leaves of Chinese
cabbage

Heat the oil in a large wok and stir-fry the Chinese mushrooms and salt for 1 minute, stirring frequently. Add the zucchini, bamboo shoots, baby corn, water chestnuts, leek, tofu, soy sauce, sugar, pepper, sesame oil, and cornstarch mixture. Stir-fry the vegetables for 1 minute, stirring frequently. Remove the vegetables from the wok and line the same large wok (after washing it) or flame proof casserole with the Chinese cabbage and pour the vegetables and reserved mushroom soaking water over the Chinese cabbage. Bring to a simmer for 5 minutes or until the vegetables are tender. Do not overcook.

*Serves 4-6.*

# BEAN CURD SHEET ROLLS

2 tablespoons canola oil

1 small yellow onion, finely chopped

4 cloves garlic, minced

8 dried black Chinese mushrooms, soaked in 1/4 cup of warm water for 10 minutes (reserve the water), cut into julienne strips (Note: Discard the hard ends from the stems.)

1/2 teaspoon salt

4 yuba sticks (dry bean curd), soaked in 2 cups of boiling water for 20 minutes, drained, thinly sliced

1 cup canned bamboo shoot strips

1 pkg. flavored dried tofu (10.5 oz.), cut into strips

1/4 cup light soy sauce

1 pkg. dried bean curd skin (6 oz.), soaked in 2 cups of warm water for 10 minutes, drained

1 tablespoon cornstarch, dissolved in 1 cup of cold water

2 teaspoons sesame oil

To prepare the filling, heat the oil in a large wok and sauté the onion and garlic until light golden brown. Add the black Chinese mushrooms and salt, then stir-fry for 1 minute, stirring frequently. Add the yuba sticks, bamboo shoots, dried tofu, and soy sauce. Simmer for 3 minutes and remove from the wok. Set the filling aside and let it cool. Place 2 tablespoons of the filling on the soaked bean curd skin about 1 inch from the edge nearest you. Lift the edge of the skin up over the filling and roll it up 2 times. Next, fold in the sides, roll it up one more time tightly and continue rolling to make a neat package. Continue making the bean curd sheet rolls until they are all ready. Place them in a large nonstick frying pan and add the reserved mushroom soaking water and cornstarch mixture. Simmer for 5 minutes and drizzle with the sesame oil.

*Serves 4-6.*

# Broccoli with Beef

1/2 lb. sirloin beef, thinly
  sliced
3 cloves garlic, minced
1 tablespoon light soy sauce
2 tablespoons oyster sauce
1 tablespoon dry sherry or
  white wine
1 teaspoon brown sugar
1 tablespoon cornstarch
3 tablespoons canola oil
1 lb. fresh broccoli, cut into
  small florets (Discard the
  tough stems.)
2 small carrots, peeled,
  thinly sliced
1/4 cup water
1/2 teaspoon salt

In a bowl, marinate the beef with garlic, soy sauce, oyster sauce, wine, sugar, and cornstarch for 10 minutes. Heat 2 tablespoons of oil in a wok over high heat and sauté the marinated beef for 2 minutes, stirring frequently. Remove the beef and set it aside. Using the same wok, heat the remaining tablespoon of oil over medium high heat and sauté the broccoli and carrots, stirring frequently for a few seconds. Reduce the heat to low and add the water and salt. Simmer for 2 minutes, stirring occasionally. Add the sautéed beef and stir well. Serve hot over white rice.

*Serves 4-6.*

# BUDDHA'S DELIGHT

6 outer leaves of head lettuce or Chinese cabbage

4 yuba sticks (dry bean curd), soaked in 2 cups of boiling water for 20 minutes, drained, cut into 2-inch lengths

1 cup cellophane noodles, soaked in warm water for 5 minutes, drained, cut into 3-inch lengths

1/4 cup lily buds, soaked in 1/2 cup warm water for 20 minutes, drained

6 dried black Chinese mushrooms, soaked in 1/2 cup of warm water for 10 minutes (reserve the water), cut in half (Note: Discard the hard ends from the stems.)

1/4 cup canned sliced bamboo shoots

1/4 cup canned sliced water chestnuts

1 pkg. fried tofu (10.5 oz.), cubed

1/4 cup light soy sauce

1/2 teaspoon salt

1 tablespoon rice wine

1 cup canned baby corn

1 cup water or chicken broth

1 cup green beans, ends removed, cut into 2-inch lengths (or use 1 cup broccoli florets)

2 teaspoons sesame oil

Line a large wok or flameproof casserole with the head lettuce leaves. Arrange in layers the yuba, cellophane noodles, lily buds, black Chinese mushrooms, bamboo shoots, water chestnuts, fried tofu, soy sauce, salt, wine, baby corn, water, and reserved mushroom soaking water. Bring the mixture to a boil, then lower the heat and simmer for 20 minutes. Add the green beans and cover. Simmer for 2 more minutes. Drizzle the sesame oil on top and serve hot, straight from the wok or casserole.

*Serves 4-6.*

# EGGPLANT WITH BLACK BEAN SAUCE

2 lbs. Japanese eggplant
2 tablespoons canola oil
2 teaspoons minced fresh
  ginger
3 cloves garlic, minced
1/4 lb. ground pork (optional)
1 tablespoon salted black
  beans (Chinese style),
  minced
1/4 teaspoon salt
1 tablespoon light soy sauce
1 teaspoon sugar
1/4 cup chicken broth or water
4 green onions, chopped

Slice the eggplants crosswise on a diagonal into 1/2-inch thick slices. Heat the oil in a large wok and stir-fry the ginger, garlic, pork, salted black beans, and salt for 2 minutes, stirring occasionally. Add the eggplant, soy sauce, and sugar, and stir-fry for a few seconds. Reduce the heat to low and add the chicken broth. Simmer for 3 minutes or until the eggplant is tender. Garnish with the green onions.

*Serves 4-6.*

# EGGPLANT WITH HOT BEAN SAUCE

1 lb. Japanese eggplant
2 tablespoons canola oil
4 cloves garlic, minced
1/4 cup light soy sauce
2 tablespoons rice wine
2 tablespoons hot bean sauce
1/2 teaspoon ground
  white pepper
4 green onions, finely
  chopped
1 teaspoon sesame oil

Slice the eggplants crosswise on a diagonal into 1/2-inch thick slices. Heat the oil in a large wok over high heat and stir-fry the garlic and eggplant for 2 minutes, stirring occasionally. Add the soy sauce, wine, bean sauce, and pepper. Reduce the heat to low and simmer for 3 minutes or until the eggplant is soft. Garnish with the green onions and drizzle with the sesame oil.

*Serves 4-6.*

# Eggplant with Chicken

2 lbs. Japanese eggplant
1/4 cup canola oil
4 cloves garlic, minced
1/2 teaspoon salt
1/2 lb. boneless chicken
  breast, thinly sliced
2 fresh red cayenne peppers,
  minced
1 teaspoon sugar
1/2 teaspoon ground white
  pepper
2 tablespoons hot bean sauce
4 green onions, chopped
1 teaspoon sesame oil

Slice the eggplant crosswise on a diagonal into 1/2-inch thick slices. Heat the oil in a large wok over high heat and add the garlic, salt, chicken, cayenne peppers, and eggplant. Stir-fry for 3 minutes, stirring occasionally. Add the sugar, pepper, and hot bean sauce and stir-fry for 2 minutes or until the chicken is cooked. Garnish with the green onions and drizzle with sesame oil.

*Serves 4-6.*

# Eggplant with Dried Tofu

4 Japanese eggplants
3 tablespoons canola oil
4 cloves garlic, minced
1 teaspoon minced fresh
  ginger
2 fresh red cayenne peppers,
  sliced
1 pkg. flavored dried tofu
  (10.5 oz.), cut into julienne
  strips
1 teaspoon salt
4 green onions, finely
  chopped
1 teaspoon sesame oil

Slice the eggplants crosswise on a diagonal into 1/2-inch thick slices. Heat the oil in a large wok and stir-fry the garlic, ginger, cayenne peppers, and eggplant for 3 minutes, stirring frequently. Add the tofu, salt, green onions, and sesame oil and stir-fry for 2 minutes, stirring frequently. Serve immediately.

*Serves 4-6.*

# HEAD LETTUCE WITH OYSTER SAUCE

2 tablespoons canola oil
4 cloves garlic, crushed
1 large head green iceberg
   lettuce, cleaned, cut into
   2-inch cubes
3 tablespoons oyster sauce
1 teaspoon ground white
   pepper
1 tablespoon light
   soy sauce

Heat the oil in a large wok and stir-fry the garlic until light brown. Add the lettuce cubes and sauté for 1 minute, stirring frequently. Add the oyster sauce, pepper, soy sauce, and stir until well blended.

*Serves 4-6.*


# LEEK WITH BEAN CURD

2 tablespoons canola oil
3 cloves garlic, minced
1 large leek, cleaned, cut
   into 2-inch julienne strips
1/2 lb. fresh mushrooms,
   sliced
1 pkg. fried tofu (10.5 oz.),
   cubed
3 tablespoons light soy sauce
1 tablespoon cornstarch,
   dissolved in 1/4 cup of
   cold water
2 teaspoons sesame oil

Heat the oil in a large wok and sauté the garlic, leek, mushrooms, and tofu for 1 minute, stirring frequently. Add the soy sauce, cornstarch mixture, and sesame oil and stir until the sauce thickens. Serve immediately.

*Serves 4-6.*

# Lotus with Black Mushrooms

2 tablespoons canola oil
3 cloves garlic, minced
1 teaspoon minced ginger
4 dried black Chinese mushrooms, soaked in 1/4 cup of warm water for 10 minutes (reserve the water), cut in half (Note: Discard the hard ends from the stems.)
1 small carrot, peeled, sliced
1 cup sliced lotus root
1 cup sliced jicama
1 small zucchini, sliced
1 red bell pepper, seeded, cubed
1 cup fresh mushrooms, cut in half
2 tablespoons rice wine
2 tablespoons light soy sauce
1 teaspoon sugar
1 tablespoon cornstarch, dissolved in 1/4 cup of cold water
1 teaspoon sesame oil

Heat the oil in a large wok and sauté the garlic and ginger until light golden brown. Add the black Chinese mushrooms and sauté for a few seconds, stirring frequently. Add the carrot, lotus root, jicama, and reserved mushroom soaking water and stir-fry for 2 minutes, stirring frequently. Add the zucchini, bell pepper, mushrooms, wine, soy sauce and sugar and simmer for 1 minute. Add the cornstarch mixture and sesame oil and stir constantly until it becomes slightly thickened.

*Serves 4-6.*

# SPICY CABBAGE

2 tablespoons canola oil
3 cloves garlic, crushed
2 teaspoons Szechwan
   peppercorns, roasted,
   crushed
8 dried whole red cayenne
   peppers
2 lbs. green cabbage,
   washed, drained, cut into
   2-inch cubes
1/2 teaspoon salt
2 teaspoons sugar
2 tablespoons light soy sauce
1 teaspoon sesame oil

Heat the oil in a large wok and sauté the garlic, peppercorns, and cayenne peppers for 1 minute. Add the cabbage, salt, sugar, and soy sauce and sauté for 2 minutes, stirring occasionally, until the cabbage is soft and crunchy. Do not overcook. Drizzle with the sesame oil.

*Serves 4-6.*

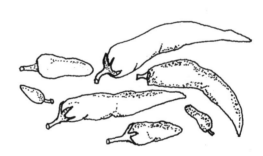

# SPICY TOFU WITH BLACK FUNGUS

2 tablespoons canola oil
3 cloves garlic, minced
1/2 teaspoon ground
 Szechwan peppercorns
1/4 cup dried black fungus
 strips soaked in warm water
 for 5 minutes, drained
2 fresh red cayenne peppers,
 minced
1 pkg. firm tofu (16 oz.),
 drained, cubed
1 tablespoon hot bean sauce
2 tablespoons light soy sauce
4 green onions, finely
 chopped
1 tablespoon cornstarch,
 dissolved in 1/4 cup of
 cold water
2 teaspoons sesame oil
1/4 cup fresh coriander
 leaves, chopped
1 small leek (white part only),
 shredded

Heat the oil in a large frying pan and stir-fry the garlic until light golden brown. Add the peppercorns, black fungus, cayenne peppers, tofu, bean sauce, and soy sauce and simmer for 5 minutes. Add the green onions, cornstarch mixture, and sesame oil and cook over low heat, stirring constantly, until the sauce thickens. Garnish with the coriander leaves and shredded leek. Serve hot over white rice.

*Serves 4-6.*

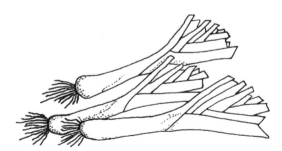

# Stir-Fried Bean Sprouts

2 tablespoons canola oil
3 cloves garlic, minced
1 fresh red cayenne pepper, sliced
2 tablespoons soy bean paste (Miso)
2 ripe tomatoes, cut into 4 wedges
1 pkg. fried tofu (10.5 oz.), cubed
1 lb. bean sprouts
4 green onions, chopped
1 teaspoon sesame oil
1/4 cup fresh coriander leaves, chopped

Heat the oil in a large wok and sauté the garlic and cayenne pepper until light golden brown. Add the soy bean paste, tomatoes, and tofu and sauté for a few seconds, stirring frequently. Add the bean sprouts, green onions, and sesame oil and stir-fry for 1 minute, stirring frequently. Garnish with the coriander leaves.

*Serves 4-6.*

# STIR-FRIED CHINESE CABBAGE

2 tablespoons canola oil
1 teaspoon minced ginger
3 cloves garlic, minced
6 dried black Chinese
mushrooms, soaked in
1/2 cup of warm water
for 10 minutes (reserve
the water), cut into julienne
strips (Note: Discard the
hard ends from the stems.)
1/2 teaspoon salt
1 small carrot, sliced
1/2 cup canned baby corn
1/2 lb. Chinese cabbage,
cut into 1-inch lengths
2 tablespoons light soy sauce
1/2 teaspoon ground white
pepper
1 tablespoon rice wine
1 can crab meat (6 1/2 oz.)
2 tablespoons cornstarch,
dissolved in 1/2 cup of
cold water
1 teaspoon sesame oil

Heat the oil in a large wok and sauté the ginger, garlic, mushrooms, and salt for a few seconds. Add the carrot, baby corn, Chinese cabbage, soy sauce, pepper, and wine for 2 minutes, stirring frequently. Add the crab meat and stir-fry for 1 minute. Add the cornstarch mixture and reserved mushroom soaking water and stir constantly until it becomes slightly thickened. Drizzle with the sesame oil.

*Serves 4-6.*

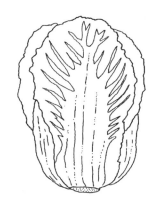

# STIR-FRIED GREEN BEANS

2 tablespoons canola oil
1 small onion, minced
1 teaspoon minced fresh
  ginger
4 cloves garlic, minced
2 fresh red cayenne peppers,
  sliced
1 lb. green beans, ends
  removed, cut into 2-inch
  lengths
2 tablespoons rice wine
1/2 teaspoon salt
4 green onions, chopped

Heat the oil in large wok and sauté the onion, ginger, garlic, and cayenne peppers until light golden brown. Add the green beans, wine, and salt and stir-fry for 2 minutes, stirring frequently. Reduce the heat to low, cover, and simmer for 3 minutes or until the green beans are tender. Do not overcook. Garnish with the green onions.

*Serves 4-6.*

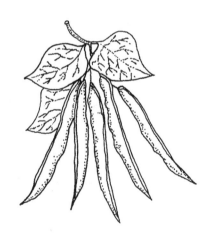

# STIR-FRIED MIXED VEGETABLES

2 tablespoons canola oil
4 cloves garlic, minced
1/2 lb. Chinese cabbage,
   cut into 1-inch squares
1/2 cup canned baby corn
1 cup canned straw
   mushrooms
1 cup canned sliced
   bamboo shoots
1/2 cup canned sliced
   water chestnuts
1 teaspoon salt
1 teaspoon sugar
1/2 teaspoon ground
   white pepper
1 tablespoon cornstarch,
   dissolved in 1/4 cup of
   cold water
1/4 cup fresh coriander
   leaves, chopped
1 teaspoon sesame oil

Heat the oil in a large wok and sauté the garlic until light golden brown. Add the Chinese cabbage and stir-fry for 2 minutes, stirring occasionally. Add the baby corn, straw mushrooms, bamboo shoots, water chestnuts, salt, sugar and pepper and stir-fry for 1 minute, stirring frequently. Add the cornstarch mixture and stir until the sauce thickens slightly. Garnish with the coriander leaves and drizzle with the sesame oil.

*Serves 4-6.*

# STIR-FRIED SPINACH

**3 tablespoons canola oil**
**1 small onion, minced**
**4 cloves garlic, minced**
**2 lbs. fresh spinach, cleaned, cut into 2-inch lengths**
**2 tablespoons oyster sauce**
**1 teaspoon sesame oil**

Heat the oil in a large wok and stir-fry the onion and garlic until golden brown. Add the spinach and stir-fry for 1 minute, stirring frequently or until the spinach wilts. Do not overcook. Add the oyster sauce and sesame oil and stir until it is all well mixed.

*Serves 4-6.*

# STIR-FRIED WATERCRESS WITH GARLIC

**3 tablespoons canola oil**
**1 small onion, minced**
**6 cloves garlic, minced**
**2 lbs. fresh watercress, cleaned, cut into 2-inch lengths**
**1/2 teaspoon ground white pepper**
**1 teaspoon salt**

Heat the oil in a large wok and sauté the onion and garlic until golden brown. Add the watercress and stir-fry for 1 minute, stirring frequently or until the watercress wilts. Do not overcook. Add the pepper and salt and stir until it is all well mixed.

*Serves 4-6.*

# STIR-FRIED WHITE ICICLE RADISH

3 tablespoons canola oil
1 small onion, minced
4 cloves garlic, minced
1/4 cup dried shrimp, soaked
   in 1/4 cup of warm water
   for 5 minutes, drained,
   (reserve the water)
2 lbs. fresh white icicle
   radish, peeled, cut into thin
   julienne strips
1 teaspoon salt
1/2 teaspoon ground white
   pepper
1 teaspoon sugar
4 green onions, finely
   chopped
1 teaspoon sesame oil

Heat the oil in a large wok and stir-fry the onion, garlic, and shrimp until light golden brown. Add the soaking shrimp water, white icicle radish, salt, pepper, and sugar. Simmer for 2 minutes, stirring occasionally, and cook until the radish is soft. Do not overcook. Garnish with the green onions and drizzle with the sesame oil.

*Serves 4-6.*

# STUFFED CUCUMBERS

1/4 cup dried shrimp, soaked in 1/4 cup of warm water for 5 minutes (discard the water), minced
1 lb. ground pork
1 teaspoon rice wine
1 teaspoon minced fresh ginger
4 green onions, minced
2 tablespoons light soy sauce
1 tablespoon cornstarch
1/2 teaspoon ground white pepper
1 egg, beaten
1 teaspoon sesame oil
3 large cucumbers, peeled, cut into 1 1/2-inch lengths, seeded

In a bowl, mix thoroughly the shrimp, pork, wine, ginger, green onions, soy sauce, cornstarch, pepper, egg, and sesame oil. Stuff the pork mixture into each seeded cucumber ring until all are done. Place them in a steamer on a damp cloth and steam them for about 20 to 25 minutes over high heat. Remove and place them on a large platter. Serve with Vinegar Sauce (see page 20).

*Serves 4-6.*

# CHAPTER SIX

# SEAFOOD

# Seafood

# ABALONE WITH BLACK MUSHROOMS

1 quart water

12 small baby bok choy

3 tablespoons canola oil

3 cloves garlic, crushed

1/2 teaspoon minced
fresh ginger

1/2 teaspoon salt

6 dried black Chinese
mushrooms, soaked in
1/4 cup of warm water
for 10 minutes (reserve
the water), cut in half
(Note: Discard the hard
ends from the stems.)

1 cup canned or fresh
abalone, thinly sliced

2 tablespoons oyster sauce

1 tablespoon cornstarch,
dissolved in 1/4 cup of
cold water

1 teaspoon sesame oil

Bring the water to a boil in a large pot. Add the baby bok choy and boil for 1 minute over high heat, then discard the water. Heat 1 tablespoon of oil in a wok and stir-fry the garlic and salt for a few seconds. Add the baby bok choy and stir-fry for 1 minute and place them on a large serving platter. Set them aside. Heat the remaining 2 tablespoons of oil in a large wok and stir-fry the ginger and black mushrooms for a few seconds. Add the reserved mushroom soaking water, abalone, oyster sauce and cornstarch mixture and stir constantly until it becomes slightly thickened. Pour the abalone mixture over the baby bok choy and drizzle with the sesame oil. Serve hot with white rice.

*Serves 4-6.*

# CLAMS WITH BLACK BEAN SAUCE

2 tablespoons canola oil
1/4 lb. ground pork
1 teaspoon minced fresh
  ginger
3 cloves garlic, minced
2 fresh red cayenne
  peppers, minced
2 tablespoons light soy sauce
4 lbs. fresh clams,
  washed, drained
1/4 cup water
1 tablespoon salted black
  beans (Chinese style),
  minced
2 green onions, cut into
  2-inch julienne strips

Heat the oil in a large wok and stir-fry the pork, ginger, garlic, and cayenne peppers for 1 minute, stirring occasionally. Add the soy sauce, clams, water, and black beans and sauté for 2 minutes, stirring frequently. Reduce the heat to low and simmer for 3 minutes or until the clams open. Discard any unopened clams. Garnish with the green onions.

*Serves 4-6.*

# STEAMED CLAMS WITH GINGER

4 lbs. fresh clams,
  washed, cleaned
1 tablespoon shredded
  fresh ginger
3 tablespoons light soy sauce
2 tablespoons rice wine
1 teaspoon sugar
2 teaspoons fresh lime juice
1/4 teaspoon ground
  white pepper
1 fresh red cayenne
  pepper, sliced (optional)
1 teaspoon canola oil
4 green onions, shredded
4 sprigs fresh coriander
  leaves, cut in half

Place the clams in a large heatproof bowl. In a small bowl, combine the ginger, soy sauce, wine, sugar, lime juice, pepper, cayenne pepper, and oil. Pour the mixture over the clams. Place the dish in a steamer and steam over high heat for 2 minutes or until the clams open. Discard any unopened clams. Garnish with the green onions and coriander leaves.

*Serves 4-6.*

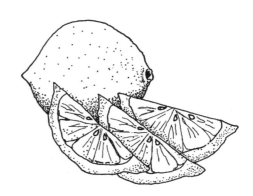

# CRAB WITH BABY BOK CHOY

1 quart water
24 small baby bok choy
3 tablespoons canola oil
3 cloves garlic, crushed
1 teaspoon salt
2 green onions, chopped
1 teaspoon minced
   fresh ginger
1 can crab meat (6 1/2 oz.)
1/2 teaspoon ground
   white pepper
1 tablespoon rice wine
2 tablespoons cornstarch,
   dissolved in 2 cups of
   cold water
1 egg white, beaten

Bring the water to a boil in a large deep pot. Add the baby bok choy and boil for 1 minute over high heat, then discard the water. Heat 2 tablespoons of oil in a large wok and sauté the garlic until light golden brown. Add the baby bok choy and salt. Stir-fry for 1 minute and place them on a large serving platter. Set them aside. Heat the remaining 1 tablespoon of oil in a large wok and sauté the green onions and ginger for a few seconds. Add the crab meat, pepper, and wine and stir-fry for 1 minute. Add the cornstarch mixture and stir constantly until it becomes slightly thickened. Next, pour the beaten egg white carefully into the sauce and stir again until well blended. Pour the crab mixture over the baby bok choy. Serve hot with white rice.

*Serves 4-6.*

# FRIED FISH WITH BLACK BEAN SAUCE

2 lbs. fillet of flounder, cut
    into 4 pieces
1/2 teaspoon salt
1/2 teaspoon ground
    white pepper
3 tablespoons cornstarch
5 tablespoons canola oil
2 tablespoons salted
    black beans, (Chinese
    style), coarsely chopped
1 one-inch piece fresh
    ginger, cut into
    julienne strips
3 cloves garlic, minced
1 small onion, finely chopped
3 tablespoons light soy sauce
3 tablespoons rice wine
2 tablespoons cornstarch,
    dissolved in 1 cup of
    cold water
4 green onions, chopped
1 teaspoon sesame oil

Place the fillets in a large bowl, rub them with salt and pepper and coat them with cornstarch on both sides. Heat 3 tablespoons of oil in a large wok over medium high heat and fry the fillets for 3 minutes on each side or until they are crispy and golden brown. Remove them and drain on paper towels. Place them on a large plate and set it aside. Heat the remaining 2 tablespoons of oil in the same wok and stir-fry the black beans, ginger, garlic and onion for 2 minutes. Add the soy sauce, wine and cornstarch mixture and stir constantly until it becomes slightly thickened. Pour the sauce over the fillets. Garnish with the green onions and drizzle with the sesame oil.

*Serves 4-6.*

# Fried Fish with Soy Bean Paste

2 lbs. fillet of flounder, cut
  into 4 pieces
1/2 teaspoon ground
  white pepper
1/4 cup cornstarch
5 tablespoons canola oil
1 teaspoon shredded
  fresh ginger
3 cloves garlic, minced
1 tablespoon light soy sauce
2 tablespoons soy bean
  paste (Miso)
2 tablespoons rice wine
2 teaspoons sugar
1 tablespoon cornstarch,
  dissolved in 1/2 cup of
  cold water
4 green onions, cut into
  2-inch julienne strips

Place the fillets in a large bowl and dust them with pepper and cornstarch on both sides. Heat 3 tablespoons of oil in a large wok over medium heat and fry the fillets for 3 minutes on each side or until they are crispy and golden brown. Remove them and drain on paper towels. Heat the remaining 2 tablespoons of oil in the same wok and stir-fry the ginger and garlic for a few seconds. Add the soy sauce, soy bean paste, wine, sugar, and cornstarch mixture and stir constantly until it becomes slightly thickened. Add the fried fillets and green onions and stir until well blended. Place them on a large serving platter and serve immediately.

*Serves 4-6.*

88

# FRIED FISH WITH TOMATO SAUCE

2 lb. whole trout,
    cleaned, scored diagonally
    on both sides 1/2-inch
    deep and 2 inches apart
1 teaspoon salt
3 tablespoons cornstarch
5 tablespoons canola oil
2 fresh red cayenne
    peppers, sliced
3 cloves garlic, minced
4 dried black Chinese
    mushrooms, soaked
    in 1/4 cup of warm water
    for 10 minutes (reserve
    the water), cut into
    julienne strips (Note:
    Discard the hard ends
    from the stems.)
2 large tomatoes,
    peeled, seeded, cubed
1 small carrot, peeled, cubed
1/4 cup frozen peas
2 tablespoons sugar
1/4 cup white vinegar
1/4 cup ketchup
2 tablespoons cornstarch,
    dissolved in 1 cup of
    cold water
2 green onions (white part
    only), cut into 2-inch strips

Place the fish in a large bowl, rub it with salt and dust it with cornstarch on both sides. Heat 3 tablespoons of oil in a large wok over medium heat and fry the fish for 3 minutes on each side or until crispy and golden brown. Remove it and drain on paper towels. Place it on a large plate and set it aside. Heat the remaining 2 tablespoons of oil in the same wok and stir-fry the cayenne peppers, garlic, and Chinese mushrooms until light golden brown. Add the tomatoes, carrot, peas, sugar, vinegar, ketchup, and reserved mushroom soaking water and simmer for 2 minutes. Add the cornstarch mixture and stir until the sauce thickens slightly. Pour the sauce over the crispy fish and garnish with the green onions.

*Serves 4-6.*

# Spicy Fried Fish with Ginger

2 lbs. fillet of flounder, cut
  into 4 pieces
1/2 teaspoon salt
1/2 teaspoon ground
  white pepper
1 egg white, beaten
3 tablespoons cornstarch
5 tablespoons canola oil
1 teaspoon shredded
  fresh ginger
6 green onions, shredded
2 fresh red cayenne
  peppers, sliced
3 tablespoons rice wine
3 tablespoons light soy sauce
1 teaspoon sugar
1 small leek (white
  part only), shredded

Place the fillets in a large bowl and rub them with salt, pepper, and egg white. Dust them with cornstarch on both sides. Heat 3 tablespoons of oil in a large wok over medium heat and fry the fillets for 3 minutes on each side or until they are crispy and golden brown. Remove them and drain them on paper towels. Place them on a large platter and set it aside. Heat the remaining 2 tablespoons of oil in the same wok and stir-fry the ginger, green onions, and cayenne peppers for a few seconds. Add the wine, soy sauce, and sugar and stir well until the sugar is dissolved. Drizzle over the fillets and garnish with the shredded leek.

*Serves 4-6.*

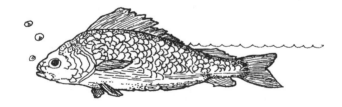

# STEAMED SEA BASS

2 lb. whole sea bass, scored
   diagonally on both sides
   1/2-inch deep and
   2-inches apart
1 teaspoon hot bean sauce
1 tablespoon salted black
   beans (Chinese style)
1 one-inch piece fresh
   ginger, cut into
   julienne strips
2 teaspoons sesame oil
4 green onions, shredded
2 tablespoons rice wine
2 tablespoons light soy sauce
1/4 cup fresh coriander leaves

Place the fish on a large heatproof plate. In a small bowl, combine the bean sauce, salted black beans, ginger, sesame oil, green onions, wine, and soy sauce. Pour the mixture on top of the fish. Put the plate of fish in a steamer and steam over high heat for 15 to 20 minutes. Garnish with the coriander leaves. Serve hot over white rice.

*Serves 4-6.*

# SPICY SQUID

3 tablespoons canola oil
4 dried red cayenne peppers
3 cloves garlic, crushed
1 lb. squid, cleaned (see
   diagram, page 143), cut
   into 2-inch lengths
1 tablespoon rice wine
1/2 teaspoon salt
2 tablespoons light soy sauce
2 teaspoons sugar
4 green onions, cut into
   2-inch lengths
1 teaspoon sesame oil

Heat the oil in a large wok and stir-fry the cayenne peppers, garlic, and squid for 1 minute, stirring constantly. Add the wine, salt, soy sauce, sugar, and green onions and stir-fry for a few seconds. Drizzle with the sesame oil.

*Serves 4-6.*

# LOBSTER IN BLACK BEAN SAUCE

**1/4 cup cornstarch**
**1/2 teaspoon salt**
**2 lb. lobster, cleaned, cut**
 **in half with the shell left on**
**3 tablespoons canola oil**
**3 cloves garlic, minced**
**1 one-inch piece fresh**
 **ginger, cut into**
 **julienne strips**
**4 green onions, cut into**
 **2-inch lengths**
**1 tablespoon salted black**
 **beans (Chinese style),**
 **coarsely chopped**
**2 tablespoons light soy sauce**
**2 tablespoons rice wine**
**1/2 teaspoon sugar**
**1 fresh red cayenne**
 **pepper, sliced (optional)**

Combine the cornstarch and salt in a large bowl and thoroughly coat the lobster by rolling it in the mixture. Heat 2 tablespoons of oil in a large wok and stir-fry the lobster for 5 minutes, stirring frequently or until it starts to turn color. Place it on a large platter and set it aside. In the same wok, heat the remaining tablespoon of oil and sauté the garlic, ginger, green onions, and black beans for a few seconds, stirring frequently. Add the soy sauce, wine, sugar, pepper, and fried lobster and stir-fry for 2 minutes, stirring frequently. Serve hot with white rice.

*Serves 4-6.*

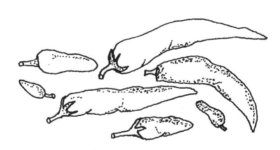

# SCALLOPS WITH ASPARAGUS

1 lb. sea scallops
1/2 teaspoon ground
   white pepper
1 egg white, beaten
1/2 teaspoon salt
2 tablespoons cornstarch
3 tablespoons canola oil
1 tablespoon minced
   fresh ginger
3 cloves garlic, minced
1/2 lb. asparagus, hard
   ends trimmed, cut into
   2-inch lengths
2 tablespoons rice wine
2 tablespoons oyster sauce

In a small bowl, marinate the scallops, pepper, egg white, salt, and cornstarch for at least 20 minutes, refrigerated. Heat 2 tablespoons of oil in a large wok and sauté the ginger and marinated scallops for a few seconds, stirring constantly. Do not overcook. Remove the scallops from the wok and set them aside. Heat the remaining tablespoon of oil in the same wok and sauté the garlic and asparagus for 1 minute, stirring frequently. Add the wine and simmer for 2 minutes or until the asparagus is tender. Stir in the cooked scallops and oyster sauce until well mixed.

*Serves 4-6.*

# Scallops with Black Mushrooms

3 tablespoons canola oil
1 small yellow onion, cut
  into quarters
8 dried black Chinese
  mushrooms, soaked
  in 1/4 cup of warm water
  for 10 minutes (reserve the
  water), cut into julienne
  strips (Note: Discard the
  hard ends from the stems.)
1/2 teaspoon salt
3 cloves garlic, minced
1 tablespoon shredded
  fresh ginger
1 lb. sea scallops, coated
  with 2 tablespoons
  cornstarch
2 tablespoons oyster sauce
6 green onions, cut into
  2-inch lengths
1 teaspoon sesame oil

Heat 1 tablespoon of oil and stir-fry the onion, Chinese mushrooms, and salt for 1 minute, stirring frequently. Remove the mushrooms from the wok and set aside. Heat the remaining 2 tablespoons of oil in the same wok and stir-fry the garlic, ginger, and scallop mixture for 1 minute, stirring constantly. Add the oyster sauce, green onions, sesame oil, reserved mushroom soaking water, and stir-fried mushrooms. Stir-fry for a few seconds or until well mixed.

*Serves 4-6.*

# SCALLOPS WITH MIXED VEGETABLES

1/2 lb. sea scallops
1/2 teaspoon ground white
   pepper
1 egg white, beaten
1/2 teaspoon salt
2 tablespoons cornstarch
3 tablespoons canola oil
3 cloves garlic, minced
1 tablespoon shredded
   fresh ginger
1/4 lb. Chinese cabbage,
   thinly sliced
1/2 cup canned bamboo
   shoots
1 carrot, peeled, thinly sliced
1/2 cup canned baby corn,
   cut in half lengthwise
1/4 cup canned straw
   mushrooms
1 teaspoon sugar
2 tablespoons light soy sauce
3 tablespoons rice wine
2 green onions, cut into
   2-inch lengths
1 teaspoon sesame oil

In a bowl, thoroughly mix the scallops, pepper, egg white, salt, and cornstarch. Heat 2 tablespoons of oil in a large wok and stir-fry the marinated scallops for a few seconds, stirring constantly. Do not overcook. Remove them from the wok and set them aside. Heat the remaining tablespoon of oil in the same wok and stir-fry the garlic and ginger until light golden brown. Add the Chinese cabbage, bamboo shoots, carrot, baby corn, straw mushrooms, sugar, soy sauce, and wine for 2 minutes, stirring occasionally. Add the cooked scallops and green onions and sauté for 1 minute, stirring frequently. Drizzle with the sesame oil. Serve hot with white rice.

*Serves 4-6.*

# KUNG PAO SHRIMP

2 lbs. shrimp, shelled,
  deveined (see diagram,
  page 145)
2 tablespoons oyster sauce
2 egg whites, beaten
3 tablespoons cornstarch
1/2 teaspoon ground
  white pepper
1 tablespoon rice wine
3 tablespoons canola oil
6 dried red cayenne peppers
1 teaspoon shredded
  fresh ginger
3 cloves garlic, minced
1 teaspoon salt
1 teaspoon sugar
6 green onions, cut
  into thin 2-inch slices
1 teaspoon sesame oil

In a large bowl, thoroughly mix the shrimp, oyster sauce, egg whites, cornstarch, pepper, and wine. Heat the oil in a large wok and stir-fry the cayenne peppers, ginger, garlic and shrimp mixture for 2 minutes, stirring frequently. Add the salt, sugar, and green onions and stir-fry for 1 minute. Drizzle with the sesame oil. Serve hot over white rice.

*Serves 4-6.*

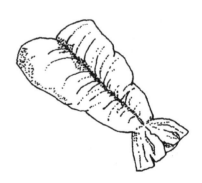

# SHRIMP WITH BLACK BEAN SAUCE

3 tablespoons canola oil
2 lbs. shrimp, shelled,
    deveined (see diagram,
    page 145)
2 teaspoons minced
    fresh ginger
5 cloves garlic, minced
2 tablespoons salted
    black beans (Chinese
    style), coarsely chopped
1 teaspoon sugar
1 tablespoon light soy sauce
3 tablespoons rice wine
6 green onions, finely
    chopped

Heat 2 tablespoons of oil in a large wok and stir-fry the shrimp for 2 minutes, stirring frequently. Remove them from the wok and set them aside. In the same wok, heat the remaining tablespoon of oil and sauté the ginger, garlic, and salted black beans for a few seconds. Add the sugar, soy sauce, wine, and green onions and stir until well blended. Add the cooked shrimp and stir-fry for 1 minute. Serve hot.

*Serves 4-6.*

# SHRIMP WITH GINGER

3 tablespoons canola oil
2 lbs. shrimp, shelled,
    deveined (see diagram,
    page 145)
3 teaspoons shredded
    fresh ginger
5 cloves garlic, minced
1 teaspoons salt
1/2 teaspoon ground
    white pepper
6 green onions, cut into
    2-inch julienne strips

Heat 2 tablespoons of oil in a large wok and stir-fry the shrimp for 2 minutes, stirring frequently. Remove them from the wok and set them aside. In the same wok, heat the remaining tablespoon of oil and sauté the ginger, garlic, salt and pepper for a few seconds. Add the stir-fried shrimp and stir-fry for 1 minute. Garnish with the green onions. Serve hot over white rice.

*Serves 4-6.*

# SHRIMP WITH SNOW PEAS

1 lb. shrimp, shelled, deveined (see diagram, page 145)
1 teaspoon salt
1 egg white, slightly beaten
2 tablespoons cornstarch
3 tablespoons canola oil
3 cloves garlic, minced
1 tablespoon shredded fresh ginger
1 lb. snow peas, ends removed, washed, drained
2 green onions, cut into 2-inch lengths
1 teaspoon sugar
2 tablespoons light soy sauce
2 tablespoons rice wine
1 teaspoon sesame oil

In a small bowl, thoroughly mix the shrimp, salt, egg white, and cornstarch. Marinate the shrimp for at least 15 minutes in the refrigerator. Heat 2 tablespoons of oil in a large wok and stir-fry the garlic, ginger, and marinated shrimp for a few seconds, stirring constantly. Do not overcook. Remove them from the wok and set them aside. Heat the remaining tablespoon of oil in the same wok and sauté the snow peas for a few seconds. Add the cooked shrimp, green onions, sugar, soy sauce, and wine and stir-fry for a few seconds, stirring frequently. Drizzle with the sesame oil. Serve hot.

*Serves 4-6.*

# SHRIMP WITH TOFU

1 lb. shrimp, shelled, deveined (see diagram, page 145)
1/2 teaspoon salt
1/4 teaspoon ground white pepper
3 tablespoons cornstarch
1 egg white, beaten
1/4 cup canola oil for frying
1 pkg. firm tofu (16 oz.), drained, cubed
2 tablespoons sesame oil
3 cloves garlic, crushed
1 teaspoon minced fresh ginger
1/2 lb. fresh mushrooms, washed, drained, sliced
2 tablespoons oyster sauce
1 teaspoon sugar
1 tablespoon soy sauce
1 tablespoon rice wine
4 green onions, finely chopped

In a small bowl, mix the shrimp, salt, pepper, cornstarch, and egg white and set the mixture aside. Heat the oil in a wok and fry the cubed tofu until golden brown on both sides. Remove the cubes, drain them on paper towels, and set them aside. Heat the sesame oil in a large frying pan and sauté the garlic and ginger until light golden brown. Add the shrimp mixture and stir-fry for 2 minutes, stirring frequently. Add the mushrooms, oyster sauce, sugar, soy sauce, wine, and fried tofu and stir-fry for a few seconds, stirring frequently. Garnish with the green onions. Serve hot over white rice.

*Serves 4-6.*

# Sweet and Sour Shrimp

2 lbs. shrimp, shelled, deveined (see diagram, page 145)
1 teaspoon salt
1 egg white, beaten
3 tablespoons cornstarch
3 tablespoons canola oil
4 cloves garlic, minced
1 fresh red cayenne pepper, sliced
1 yellow onion, sliced
1 small carrot, thinly sliced
1 red bell pepper, seeded, thinly sliced
1/2 cup sliced canned water chestnuts
1/2 cup sliced canned bamboo shoots
1/4 cup ketchup
3 tablespoons rice vinegar
1 tablespoon sugar
2 tablespoons cornstarch, dissolved in 1/2 cup of cold water
1/4 cup fresh coriander leaves, chopped
1 teaspoon sesame oil

In a small bowl, thoroughly mix the shrimp, salt, egg white, and 3 tablespoons of cornstarch. Heat 2 tablespoons of oil in a large wok and stir-fry the marinated shrimp for a few seconds, stirring constantly. Do not overcook. Remove them from the wok and set them aside. Heat the remaining tablespoon of oil in the same wok and stir-fry the garlic, cayenne pepper, onion, carrot, bell pepper, water chestnuts, and bamboo shoots for 2 minutes, stirring occasionally. Add the ketchup, vinegar, sugar, and cornstarch mixture and simmer for 1 minute. Add the stir-fried shrimp and garnish with the coriander leaves. Drizzle with the sesame oil. Serve hot.

*Serves 4-6.*

# Sweet and Spicy Shrimp

2 lbs. shrimp, shelled,
deveined (see diagram,
page 145)
1 teaspoon salt
1 egg white, beaten
3 tablespoons cornstarch
3 tablespoons canola oil
4 cloves garlic, minced
3 fresh red cayenne
peppers, sliced
1 teaspoon minced fresh
ginger
1 cup canned baby corn
1 red bell pepper, seeded,
thinly sliced
1/2 cup sliced canned
water chestnuts
1 tablespoon sugar
2 tablespoons cornstarch,
dissolved in 1/2 cup
of cold water
1/4 cup fresh coriander
leaves, chopped
4 green onions, cut into
2-inch julienne strips

In a small bowl, thoroughly mix the shrimp, salt, egg white, and 3 tablespoons of cornstarch. Heat 2 tablespoons of oil in a large wok and stir-fry the marinated shrimp for a few seconds, stirring constantly. Do not overcook. Remove them from the wok and set them aside. Heat the remaining tablespoon of oil in the same wok and stir-fry the garlic, cayenne peppers, ginger, baby corn, bell pepper, and water chestnuts for 2 minutes, stirring occasionally. Add the sugar and cornstarch mixture and simmer for 1 minute. Add the stir-fried shrimp and garnish with the coriander leaves and green onions. Serve hot over white rice.

*Serves 4-6.*

# SZECHWAN SHRIMP

2 lbs. large shrimp, heads removed, washed, drained, and dried on paper towels
1 teaspoon cayenne powder
1 teaspoon coarse sea salt
4 dried red cayenne peppers, chopped
2 teaspoons Szechwan peppercorns, crushed
5 cloves garlic, minced
3 tablespoons canola oil
4 green onions, finely chopped

In a large bowl, thoroughly mix the shrimp, cayenne powder, salt, cayenne peppers, peppercorns, and garlic. Heat the oil in a large wok and stir-fry the shrimp for 3 minutes or until the shrimp are pink and cook throughout. Place on a plate and garnish with the green onions. Serve hot.

*Serves 4-6.*

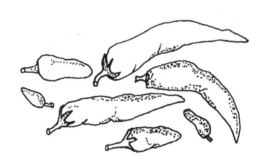

# CHAPTER SEVEN

# MEAT
# &
# POULTRY

# CHAPTER SEVEN
## Meat and Poultry

# BEEF WITH BELL PEPPERS

1/2 lb. top sirloin beef, cut
  into julienne strips
1 tablespoon light soy sauce
2 tablespoons oyster sauce
1 tablespoon rice wine
1/4 teaspoon salt
2 tablespoons cornstarch
3 tablespoons canola oil
1 one-inch piece fresh
  ginger, shredded
1 green bell pepper,
  seeded, shredded
1 red bell pepper, seeded,
  shredded
1 yellow bell pepper,
  seeded, shredded
1 teaspoon sugar
2 green onions (white
  part only), shredded

In a large bowl, marinate the beef with soy sauce, oyster sauce, wine, salt, and cornstarch for at least 20 minutes, refrigerated. Heat 2 tablespoons of oil in a large wok and stir-fry the beef mixture for 2 minutes, stirring frequently. Remove it from the wok and set it aside. Heat the remaining tablespoon of oil in the same wok and stir-fry the ginger, green bell pepper, red bell pepper, yellow bell pepper, and sugar for 1 minute, stirring frequently. Add the fried beef and stir until well blended. Garnish with the shredded green onions.

*Serves 4-6.*

# Beef with Black Bean Sauce

2 tablespoons canola oil
1 one-inch piece fresh
 ginger, shredded
1/2 lb. top sirloin beef, cut
 into thin julienne strips
2 red cayenne peppers,
 cut into julienne strips
1 tablespoon salted black
 beans (Chinese
 style), minced
1 small leek, cut into 2-inch
 julienne strips
3 stalks celery, cut into
 2-inch julienne strips
2 teaspoons brown sugar
2 teaspoons rice wine
2 teaspoons sesame oil

Heat the oil in a large wok and stir-fry the ginger, beef, cayenne peppers, and salted black beans for 1 minute, stirring occasionally. Add the leek, celery, sugar, wine, and sesame oil and stir-fry for 2 minutes. Serve hot over rice.

*Serves 4-6.*

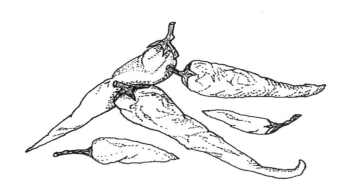

# BEEF WITH BROCCOLI

1/2 lb. top sirloin beef,
   thinly sliced
1 teaspoon rice wine
1 tablespoon oyster sauce
1/2 teaspoon sugar
1 tablespoon cornstarch
5 tablespoons canola oil
4 cloves garlic, minced
1 lb. fresh broccoli,
   cut into small florets
   (Discard the tough stems.)
1 tablespoon cornstarch,
   dissolved in 1/2 cup of
   cold water
1 teaspoon salt
1 teaspoon sesame oil

In a small bowl, mix the beef, wine, oyster sauce, sugar, and cornstarch. Heat 3 tablespoons of oil in a large wok and stir-fry the beef mixture for a few seconds, stirring frequently. Remove the beef from the wok and set it aside. Clean the wok and heat the remaining 2 tablespoons of oil and stir-fry the garlic and broccoli for 3 minutes over low heat, stirring frequently. Add the cornstarch mixture, salt, and sesame oil and stir until it thickens slightly. Add the cooked beef and mix well. Place on a large platter and serve hot.

*Serves 4-6.*

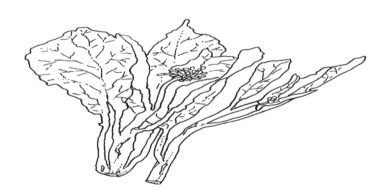

# BEEF WITH CURRIED SPICIES

2 tablespoons canola oil
3 cloves garlic, minced
2 fresh red cayenne
  peppers, minced
1 yellow onion, chopped
1 lb. top sirloin beef,
  cut into 1-inch cubes
1/4 cup curry powder
1/4 cup light soy sauce
1 tablespoon rice wine
1 tablespoon brown sugar
2 cups water
4 green onions, chopped
1/4 cup fresh coriander
  leaves, chopped

Heat the oil in a large pot and stir-fry the garlic, cayenne peppers, and onion until light golden brown. Add the beef, curry powder, soy sauce, wine, and sugar and stir-fry for 2 minutes, stirring occasionally. Add the water and simmer for 30 minutes or until the beef is tender. Garnish with the green onions and coriander leaves.

*Serves 4-6.*

# BEEF WITH OYSTER SAUCE

1 lb. top sirloin beef, thinly
  sliced
1 tablespoon rice wine
1/2 teaspoon ground
  white pepper
3 tablespoons oyster sauce
2 tablespoons canola oil
3 cloves garlic, minced
1 lb. fresh mushrooms,
  washed, drained, sliced
4 green onions, chopped
1 teaspoon sesame oil

In a small bowl, marinate the beef with wine, pepper and oyster sauce for 10 minutes in a refrigerator. Heat the oil in a wok and stir-fry the garlic and marinated beef for 2 minutes. Add the mushrooms and stir-fry for 1 minute. Garnish with the green onions and drizzle with the sesame oil.

*Serves 4-6.*

# Garlic Beef with Onion

1 lb. top sirloin beef,
   thinly sliced
1/4 teaspoon salt
1/2 teaspoon ground
   white pepper
1 teaspoon brown sugar
1 tablespoon light soy sauce
1 teaspoon rice wine
2 tablespoons cornstarch
3 tablespoons canola oil
6 cloves garlic, minced
1 large yellow onion,
   thinly sliced
2 tablespoons oyster sauce
1/4 cup fresh coriander
   leaves, chopped

In a small bowl, marinate the beef with salt, pepper, sugar, soy sauce, wine, and cornstarch for 10 minutes in a refrigerator. Heat the oil in a large wok and stir-fry the garlic and onion until light brown. Add the marinated beef and stir-fry for 2 minutes, stirring occasionally. Add the oyster sauce and stir well. Garnish with the coriander leaves.

*Serves 4-6.*

# Ginger Beef with Pineapple

1 lb. tenderloin beef or top
   sirloin steak, cut into 1/4
   inch strips
1 one-inch piece fresh ginger,
   cut into julienne strips
1 tablespoon light soy sauce
1 tablespoon dry sherry
1 tablespoon cornstarch
2 tablespoons canola oil
3 cloves garlic, minced
2 red bell peppers, seeded,
   thinly sliced
1 cup canned pineapple
   chunks
1/2 teaspoon salt
4 green onions, chopped

In a small bowl, marinate the beef with ginger, soy sauce, sherry, and cornstarch for 10 minutes in a refrigerator. Heat the oil in a wok over medium high heat. Stir-fry the marinated beef with garlic for 2 minutes, stirring occasionally. Add the peppers, pineapple, and salt and stir-fry for 1 minute, stirring frequently. Garnish with the green onions. Serve hot over rice.

*Serves 4-6.*

# MONGOLIAN BEEF

1 lb. top sirloin beef,
  thinly sliced
2 teaspoons rice wine
1 tablespoon light soy sauce
1 teaspoon sesame oil
1/2 teaspoon ground
  white pepper
2 tablespoons cornstarch
2 cups canola oil for
  deep-frying
1 pkg. (2 oz.) rice vermicelli
3 tablespoons canola oil
3 cloves garlic, minced
2 tablespoons hoisin sauce
1 tablespoon hot bean sauce
10 green onions, cut
  into 2-inch lengths

In a small bowl, mix the beef, wine, soy sauce, sesame oil, pepper, and cornstarch. Marinate the beef for at least 1 hour in a refrigerator. Heat the 2 cups of oil in a large wok over high heat. Test to see if the oil is the correct temperature by dropping a little vermicelli into it. If it puffs up white, it is good for deep-frying the vermicelli. If it doesn't puff up, the oil is not hot enough. If the oil is too hot, the vermicelli will turn a dark brown. Once you are sure the oil is the correct temperature, deep-fry the rice vermicelli in handfuls. (Do not soak the vermicelli: use it straight from the package.) Remove the puffed vermicelli from the wok with a slotted spoon, drain it on paper towels, and place it on a large platter. Repeat the same procedure until all the rice vermicelli is done. Next, heat the 3 tablespoons of oil in another wok and sauté the garlic and marinated beef for 1 minute, stirring frequently. Add the hoisin sauce, bean sauce, and green onions and stir-fry for a few seconds. Pour the beef mixture on top of the fried rice vermicelli. Serve immediately.

*Serves 4-6.*

# SZECHWAN BEEF

1 lb. top sirloin, thinly sliced
2 tablespoons light soy sauce
1 teaspoon sesame oil
2 tablespoons dry sherry
1 tablespoon hoisin sauce
1 tablespoon cornstarch
3 tablespoons canola oil
3 cloves garlic, minced
1 tablespoon hot bean sauce
1 teaspoon sugar
2 teaspoons Szechwan peppercorns, roasted, ground
4 dried whole red cayenne peppers
4 green onions, chopped

In a small bowl, marinate the beef with soy sauce, sesame oil, sherry, hoisin sauce, and cornstarch for 10 minutes. Heat the oil in a wok over high heat and stir-fry the garlic and marinated beef for 3 minutes, stirring frequently. Add the hot bean sauce, sugar, and peppercorns, cayenne peppers and stir-fry for 1 minute or until well blended. Garnish with the green onions.

*Serves 4-6.*

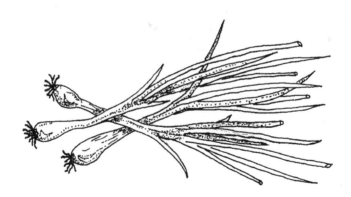

# CHICKEN BREAST WITH CASHEWS

1 lb. boneless chicken breast,
   skinned, cubed
1 teaspoon salt
1 egg white
1 tablespoon rice wine
1/2 teaspoon ground
   white pepper
2 tablespoons cornstarch
3 tablespoons canola oil
4 cloves garlic, minced
2 cups fresh mushrooms,
   quartered
3 tablespoons oyster sauce
6 green onions, cut
   into 1-inch lengths
1 cup unsalted roasted
   cashew nuts

In a small bowl, thoroughly mix the chicken, salt, egg white, wine, pepper, and cornstarch. Heat 2 tablespoons of oil and stir-fry the chicken mixture for 3 minutes, stirring frequently. Remove the chicken from the wok and set it aside. In the same wok, heat the remaining tablespoon of oil and stir-fry the garlic, mushrooms, oyster sauce, and green onions for 2 minutes, stirring frequently. Add the fried chicken and cashew nuts, stir for a few seconds, and serve hot over white rice.

*Serves 4-6.*

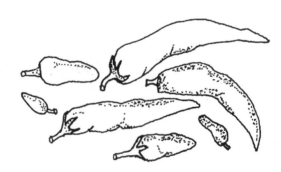

# CHICKEN IN A BIRD'S NEST

1 large potato, peeled, cut
    into thin julienne strips,
    rinsed with cold water,
    drained, tossed with
    1/2 cup of cornstarch
3 cups canola oil for
    deep-frying the potato
3 leaves of green-leaf
    lettuce, shredded
1/2 lb. boneless chicken
    breast, skinned, cubed
3 tablespoons cornstarch
1 egg white, beaten
3 tablespoons canola oil
3 cloves garlic, minced
1 small carrot, peeled, diced
1/2 cup cubed green
    bell pepper
1/2 cup cubed red bell pepper
1/2 cup canned water
    chestnuts, sliced
1 teaspoon salt
1 tablespoon cornstarch,
    dissolved in 1 cup
    of cold water
1 teaspoon sesame oil

Make sure each potato shred is coated with the cornstarch. Place the potato mixture in a large 6-inch metal strainer with a long handle; place another strainer of the same size on top. Press the potato mixture between the 2 strainers. Heat the 3 cups of oil in a large wok over high heat. Submerge the strainers in the hot oil and deep-fry the potato nest for 5 minutes or until the shreds are crispy and golden brown. Let them cool between the strainers on a paper towel about 5 minutes. Remove the nest from the strainers and place it upright on a bed of shredded lettuce on a platter. In a small bowl, mix the chicken cubes with the 3 tablespoons of cornstarch and add the egg white. In another wok, heat 2 tablespoons of oil and sauté the chicken mixture for 1 minute or until lightly browned. Remove it and set it aside. In the same wok, heat the remaining tablespoon of oil and stir-fry the garlic, carrot, green pepper, red pepper, and water chestnuts for 3 minutes, stirring occasionally. Add the salt and cornstarch mixture. Stir well until well blended. Add the sautéed chicken and sesame oil. Gently spoon the chicken mixture into the potato nest.

*Serves 4-6.*

# CHICKEN WITH ASPARAGUS

1/2 lb. boneless chicken
   breast, skinned, thinly
   sliced
1/2 teaspoon salt
1/2 teaspoon ground
   white pepper
1 tablespoon cornstarch
3 tablespoons canola oil
3 cloves garlic, minced
1 lb. fresh asparagus,
   hard ends trimmed, cut
   into 2-inch lengths
2 tablespoons light soy sauce
2 tablespoons rice wine
2 teaspoons sesame oil

In a small bowl, thoroughly mix the chicken, salt, pepper, and cornstarch. Heat 2 tablespoons of oil in a large wok and stir-fry the chicken mixture for 2 minutes, stirring frequently. Remove the chicken mixture from the wok and set it aside. In the same wok, heat the remaining tablespoon of oil and stir-fry the garlic and asparagus for 1 minute, stirring frequently. Add the soy sauce and wine and simmer for 1 minute or until the asparagus is just tender. Add the stir-fried chicken and sesame oil and stir-fry for a few seconds. Serve hot over white rice.

*Serves 4-6.*

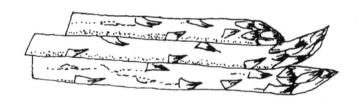

# CHICKEN WITH BLACK BEAN SAUCE

2 tablespoons canola oil
2 lbs. drumsticks
5 cloves garlic, minced
1 tablespoon, salted
  black beans (Chinese
  style), chopped
1/4 cup light soy sauce
1 tablespoon sugar
2 tablespoons rice wine
2 cups water
4 green onions, cut
  into 2-inch lengths

Heat the oil in a medium pot and stir-fry the drumsticks for 2 minutes or until light golden brown. Add the garlic and black beans and stir-fry for 1 minute, stirring occasionally. Add the soy sauce, sugar, wine, water, and green onions and reduce the heat to low. Cover and simmer for 40 minutes or until only 1/2 cup of sauce remains and the drumsticks are cooked throughout. Serve hot over rice.

*Serves 4-6.*

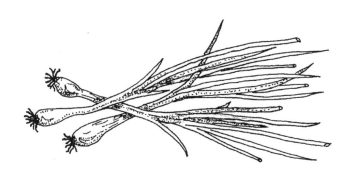

# GARLIC CHICKEN

2 lbs. boneless chicken
  breast, skinned, cubed
1 tablespoon rice wine
1 tablespoon light soy sauce
1 egg white
3 tablespoons cornstarch
5 tablespoons canola oil
8 cloves garlic, minced
2 fresh red cayenne
  peppers, sliced
1/2 cup canned sliced
  bamboo shoots
1/2 cup canned sliced
  water chestnuts
1 small carrot, peeled, sliced
1 teaspoon salt
1 teaspoon sugar
1 teaspoon sesame oil
4 green onions, cut
  into 2-inch lengths

In a small bowl, mix the chicken cubes with wine, soy sauce, egg white, and cornstarch. Heat 3 tablespoons of oil in a large wok and stir-fry the chicken cubes for 3 minutes, stirring occasionally. Remove them and set them aside. Heat the remaining 2 tablespoons of oil in the same wok and stir-fry the garlic and cayenne peppers until light brown. Add the bamboo shoots, water chestnuts, carrot, salt, sugar, and sesame oil and stir-fry for 2 minutes, stirring occasionally. Stir in the stir-fried chicken cubes and green onions.

*Serves 4-6.*

# KUNG PAO CHICKEN

1 lb. boneless chicken breast, skinned, cut into 1-inch cubes
1/2 teaspoon salt
1/2 teaspoon ground white pepper
1 egg white, beaten
2 tablespoons cornstarch
3 tablespoons canola oil
6 dried whole red cayenne peppers
3 cloves garlic, minced
1 tablespoon hot bean sauce
1 tablespoon hoisin sauce
2 tablespoons rice wine
1/2 cup cashew nuts, roasted
4 green onions, cut into 2-inch lengths
2 teaspoons sesame oil

In a small bowl, thoroughly mix the chicken, salt, pepper, egg white, and cornstarch. Heat the oil in a large wok and stir-fry the cayenne peppers, garlic, and chicken mixture for 2 minutes, stirring frequently. Add the bean sauce, hoisin sauce, and wine and stir-fry for 1 minute, stirring frequently. Add the cashew nuts, green onions, and sesame oil and stir for a few seconds.

*Serves 4-6.*

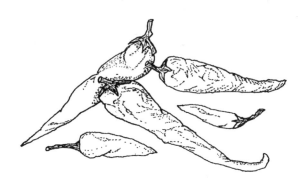

# LEMON CHICKEN

2 lbs. boneless chicken
   breast, skinned, cut
   into thin fillets
3 tablespoons rice wine
1/2 teaspoon salt
1/2 teaspoon ground
   white pepper
1 1/4 cups flour
1 large egg, beaten
2/3 cup water
1 teaspoon baking powder
2 cups canola oil for
   deep-frying
1 cup chicken broth
juice of 1 lemon
1 teaspoon grated lemon peel
2 tablespoons sugar
3 tablespoons cornstarch,
   dissolved in 1/4 cup
   of cold water
1 small lemon, cut into
   4 wedges
1/4 cup fresh coriander
   leaves

In a large bowl, marinate the chicken with wine, salt, and pepper for at least 30 minutes, or overnight, refrigerated. In a small bowl, mix the flour, egg, water, and baking powder into a smooth batter. Heat the oil in a large wok until the oil is medium hot. Coat the marinated chicken with the batter and deep-fry it for 3 minutes or until golden brown on both sides. Remove it and drain it on paper towels. Next, cut it into 1-inch strips and arrange them on a serving platter. Set it aside. In a small pot, combine the chicken broth, lemon juice, lemon peel, sugar and cornstarch mixture. Stir well and bring it to a simmer, stirring constantly, until it thickens to slightly smooth. Pour the lemon sauce over the fried chicken. Garnish with the lemon wedges and coriander leaves.

*Serves 4-6.*

# PEPPERED BARBECUED CHICKEN

8 cloves garlic, minced

1 teaspoon Szechwan peppercorns, roasted, crushed

juice of 1 lime

1 tablespoon brown sugar

1 fresh red cayenne pepper, chopped

1/4 cup hoisin sauce

1 tablespoon rice wine

1 tablespoon light soy sauce

4 lbs. drumsticks

In a large bowl, thoroughly mix the garlic, peppercorns, lime, sugar, cayenne, hoisin sauce, wine, soy sauce, and drumsticks. Marinate for at least 30 minutes, or overnight, refrigerated. Barbecue over a moderate charcoal fire for 30 minutes or until well cooked throughout. Serve with white rice and salad.

*Serves 6-8.*

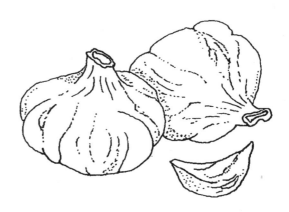

# SIZZLING CHICKEN POT

6 boneless chicken thighs, skinned, cut into 1-inch cubes

1/2 teaspoon minced ginger

1/4 teaspoon salt

2 tablespoons cornstarch

2 tablespoons canola oil

3 cloves garlic, minced

4 dried black Chinese mushrooms, soaked in 1 cup of warm water for 10 minutes (reserve the water), cut in half (Note: Discard the hard ends from the stems.)

3 tablespoons oyster sauce

2 tablespoons rice wine

2 tablespoons light soy sauce

1/2 teaspoon five-spice powder

1/2 lb. Chinese cabbage, cut into 2-inch squares

6 green onions, cut into 2-inch lengths

1 teaspoon sesame oil

In a small bowl, mix the chicken cubes with ginger, salt, and cornstarch. Heat the oil in a large wok and stir-fry the garlic and mushrooms for a few seconds. Add the marinated chicken cubes and stir-fry for 2 minutes, stirring constantly until golden brown on both sides. Add the oyster sauce, wine, soy sauce, five-spice powder, and reserved mushroom soaking water and simmer for 30 minutes or until the chicken is tender. Add the Chinese cabbage, green onions, and sesame oil and simmer again for 5 minutes or until the cabbage is tender. Do not overcook the Chinese cabbage.

*Serves 4-6.*

# Spicy Chicken

4 lbs. drumsticks
1/4 cup soy sauce
3 tablespoons rice wine
1/2 teaspoon ground
  white pepper
2 tablespoons fresh
  lemon juice
1/2 cup cornstarch
2 cups canola oil for
  deep-frying
2 tablespoons sesame oil
8 green onions, chopped
3 fresh red cayenne peppers,
  chopped

In a large bowl, combine the drumsticks with soy sauce, wine, pepper, and lemon juice. Marinate the drumsticks for 30 minutes, or overnight, refrigerated. On a plate, coat the drumsticks with cornstarch. In a large wok, heat the oil and fry the drumsticks for 5 minutes on each side or until crispy golden brown and cooked throughout. Remove them from the wok and set them aside. In a small pot, heat the sesame oil and stir-fry the green onions and cayenne peppers for a few seconds, stirring frequently. Place the drumsticks on a large plate and pour the green onion mixture over them.

*Serves 4-6.*

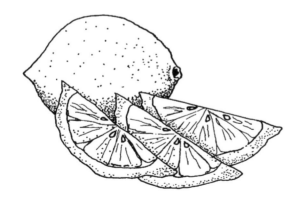

# CRISPY ROAST DUCK

4 quarts water
3-4 lb. whole duck
1/2 teaspoon salt
2 teaspoons Chinese
    five-spice powder
1/2 tablespoon honey
1/2 tablespoon brown sugar
3 tablespoons light soy sauce
1 teaspoon minced
    fresh ginger
1 green onion, cut into
    2-inch lengths

Bring the water to a boil in a large deep pot. Remove the pot from the heat and dunk the duck briefly in the hot water. Drain and dry the duck with paper towels. Rub the duck all over with salt and five-spice powder. Place the duck on a roasting rack set it in a shallow roasting pan. In a small bowl, mix the honey, sugar, soy sauce, ginger, and green onion. Brush the duck all over with the sauce. Bake, uncovered, in a 450 degree oven for 15 minutes, reduce the oven temperature to 350 degrees, and bake for 1 hour, or until the duck is cooked throughout and crispy golden brown on both sides. Make sure to baste the duck with the sauce every 15 minutes. Remove the duck from the oven. Let it stand for 10 minutes. Cut the duck into small bite-sized pieces. Serve hot with Hot Hoisin Sauce (see page 16).

*Serves 4-6.*

# Roast Leg of Lamb

1 one-inch piece fresh ginger, thinly sliced
8 cloves garlic, minced
1/2 cup rice wine
1/4 cup hoisin sauce
1/4 cup light soy sauce
2 teaspoons ground Szechwan peppercorns, crushed
4 whole star anise
4-6 lb. leg of lamb

In a large bowl, mix the ginger, garlic, wine, hoisin sauce, soy sauce, Szechwan peppercorns, and star anise. Add the lamb and marinate for at least 40 minutes, or overnight, refrigerated. Put the lamb in a large roasting pan and pour the mixture over it. Bake, covered, about 2 hours in a preheated oven at 350 degrees. Uncover and bake for 30 more minutes or until the top is golden brown. Let it cool for 15 minutes before carving.

*Serves 6-8.*

# Mu Shu Pork

3 tablespoons canola oil
2 eggs, well beaten
3 cloves garlic, minced
1 lb. tenderloin pork, cut
   into thin julienne strips
1/2 teaspoon salt
1/2 teaspoon ground
   white pepper
1/4 cup dried black fungus
   strips, soaked in warm
   water for 5 minutes,
   washed, drained
2 cups shredded
   Chinese cabbage
1/2 cup canned sliced
   bamboo shoots, cut
   into julienne strips
2 tablespoons light soy sauce
1 teaspoon sugar
1 tablespoon rice wine
4 green onions, chopped
2 teaspoons sesame oil
10 Chinese pancakes
   (see page 25) or 6-inch
   white flour tortilla shells
Hot Hoisin Sauce (see
   page 16)

Heat 1 tablespoon of oil in a large wok. Add the beaten eggs and scramble them, stirring until the eggs are just set, for approximately 1 minute. Remove the scrambled eggs from the wok and set them aside. In the same wok, heat the remaining 2 tablespoons of oil over high heat and stir-fry the garlic, pork, salt, and pepper for 3 minutes, stirring frequently. Add the fungus, Chinese cabbage, bamboo shoots, soy sauce, sugar, and wine and stir-fry for 2 minutes, stirring occasionally. Add the scrambled eggs, green onions and sesame oil. Serve the pork mixture rolled in pancake packages with Hot Hoisin Sauce on the side. The same mixture is used for chicken, shrimp or fried tofu.

*Serves 4-6.*

# PORK WITH BLACK FUNGUS

1/2 lb. tenderloin pork, cut
  into thin julienne strips
2 tablespoons light soy sauce
2 tablespoons cornstarch
3 tablespoons canola oil
1 teaspoon minced
  fresh ginger
3 cloves garlic, minced
1 cup canned sliced water
  chestnuts, cut into
  julienne strips
1/4 cup dried black fungus
  strips, soaked in warm
  water for 5 minutes,
  washed, drained
1 tablespoon rice wine
1 teaspoon sugar
1/2 teaspoon ground
  black pepper
1/2 teaspoon salt
1 tablespoon hot bean sauce
4 green onions, finely
  chopped
1 teaspoon sesame oil

In a large bowl, marinate the pork, soy sauce, and cornstarch for at least 20 minutes, refrigerated. Heat 2 tablespoons of oil in a large wok and stir-fry the ginger and pork mixture for 3 minutes, stirring frequently. Remove it and set it aside. Heat the remaining tablespoon of oil in the same wok and stir-fry the garlic, water chestnuts, black fungus strips, wine, sugar, pepper, salt, and bean sauce for 1 minute, stirring frequently. Add the stir-fried pork and green onions and stir until well blended. Drizzle with the sesame oil. Serve hot over white rice.

*Serves 4-6.*

# Sweet and Sour Pork

1 lb. pork tenderloin, cut
   into 1-inch cubes
1 egg white, beaten
3 tablespoons cornstarch
1/2 teaspoon salt
1/2 teaspoon ground
   white pepper
2 cups canola oil for
   deep-frying
1 tablespoon canola oil
3 cloves garlic, minced
1 green bell pepper,
   seeded, cut into
   1-inch cubes
1 red bell pepper, seeded,
   cut into 1-inch cubes
1 cup canned pineapple
   chunks
2 tablespoons white vinegar
2 tablespoons sugar
1/4 cup ketchup
1/2 teaspoon salt
2 tablespoons cornstarch,
   dissolved in 1/2 cup of
   cold water
1 teaspoon sesame oil

In a small bowl, mix the pork and egg white. Coat the pork cubes with the 3 tablespoons cornstarch, salt, and pepper on both sides. Heat the oil in a wok and deep-fry the pork cubes until golden brown. Remove the crispy pork cubes from the wok. Drain them on paper towels and set them aside. Heat the remaining tablespoon of oil in the same wok and stir-fry the garlic, green bell pepper, red bell pepper, and pineapple for 1 minute, stirring frequently. Add the vinegar, sugar, ketchup, salt, and cornstarch mixture, stirring constantly until the sauce loosely thickens. Add the crispy pork cubes. Drizzle with the sesame oil. Serve hot.

*Serves 4-6.*

# RICE
# &
# NOODLES

# CHAPTER EIGHT
## Rice and Noodles

# GLUTINOUS RICE

**2 cups glutinous rice,
washed, soaked overnight,
drained**

Line a large steamer with a damp cloth and place the glutinous rice into it. Cover and steam over a high heat for 20 minutes or until the rice is just soft. Remove it from the steamer and serve it warm.

*Serves 4-6.*

# LONG-GRAIN WHITE RICE

**2 cups long-grain rice,
washed, drained
3 cups water
1/4 teaspoon salt**

In a large uncovered pot, bring the rice, water and salt to a boil over high heat for 3 minutes, stirring occasionally. Reduce the heat to low and cover the pot. Simmer for 20 minutes or until the rice is soft. Remove the rice from the pot and serve it warm.

*Serves 4-6.*

# Stir-Fried Glutinous Rice

2 tablespoons canola oil
1 small onion, chopped
4 cloves garlic, minced
8 dried black Chinese
  mushrooms, soaked in 1/4
  cup of warm water for 10
  minutes (reserve the water),
  cut into julienne strips
  (Note: Discard the hard
  ends from the stems.)
1/4 teaspoon salt
1/2 teaspoon ground
  white pepper
1/4 lb. pork loin, cut into
  julienne strips
2 teaspoons five-spice
  powder
2 teaspoons sesame oil
2 tablespoons light soy sauce
3 cups cooked glutinous rice
  (see page 129)
1/4 cup fresh coriander
  leaves, chopped

Heat the oil in a large wok and stir-fry the onion and garlic until light golden brown. Add the black Chinese mushrooms, salt, and pepper and stir-fry for 1 minute, stirring frequently. Add the pork, five-spice powder, and sesame oil, and stir-fry for 3 minutes, stirring frequently. Add the reserved mushroom water and soy sauce and simmer for 2 minutes, stirring occasionally. Add the rice and stir well until all mixed. Garnish with the coriander leaves.

*Serves 4-6.*

# PORK CHOW MEIN

2 tablespoons canola oil
3 cloves garlic, crushed
1 small onion, chopped
1/2 lb. tenderloin pork,
  thinly sliced
2 small carrots, peeled,
  thinly sliced
1/4 lb. green cabbage, cut
  into 1-inch cubes
1/4 cup oyster sauce
1 tablespoon light soy sauce
1/2 teaspoon ground
  white pepper
1 lb. cooked egg noodles
4 green onions, cut
  into 1-inch lengths
1/4 cup fresh coriander
  leaves, chopped
2 teaspoons sesame oil

Heat the oil in a large wok and stir-fry the garlic and onion until light golden brown. Add the pork and stir-fry for 3 minutes, stirring occasionally. Add the carrots, cabbage, oyster sauce, soy sauce, pepper, and noodles and stir-fry for 2 minutes or until the vegetables are cooked. Add the green onions and stir-fry for a few seconds. Garnish with the coriander leaves and drizzle with the sesame oil.

*Serves 4-6.*

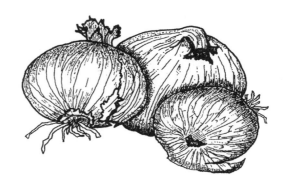

# SHRIMP CHOW MEIN

2 tablespoons canola oil
3 cloves garlic, crushed
1 small onion, chopped
1 lb. medium shrimp,
    shelled, deveined (see
    diagram, page 145)
1 large carrot, peeled,
    thinly sliced
1 lb. bean sprouts,
    washed, drained
1 stalk celery, thinly
    sliced diagonally
1/4 cup oyster sauce
1 teaspoon brown sugar
1 tablespoon light soy sauce
1/2 teaspoon ground
    white pepper
1 lb. cooked egg noodles
4 green onions, chopped
1/4 cup fresh coriander
    leaves, chopped

Heat the oil in a large wok and stir-fry the garlic and onion until light golden brown. Add the shrimp and carrot and stir-fry for 2 minutes, stirring frequently. Add the bean sprouts, celery, oyster sauce, sugar, soy sauce, pepper, and noodles and stir-fry for 2 more minutes, stirring frequently or until well mixed. Garnish with the green onions and coriander leaves. Serve hot.

*Serves 4-6.*

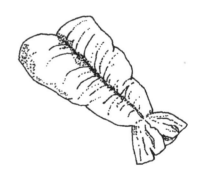

# STIR-FRIED CURRIED VEGETABLE RICE

2 tablespoons canola oil
3 cloves garlic, crushed
1 small onion, chopped
1 fresh red cayenne
  pepper, chopped
1 tablespoon curry powder
1 large carrot, peeled,
  finely cubed
1 cup frozen peas
1 small leek (white part only),
  finely chopped
3 cups cooked long-grain
  rice (see page 129)
1 teaspoon salt
1/2 teaspoon ground
  white pepper
1 tablespoon light soy sauce
4 green onions, chopped
1/4 cup fresh coriander
  leaves, chopped

Heat the oil in a large wok and stir-fry the garlic, onion, and cayenne pepper for a few seconds or until light golden brown. Add the curry, carrot, peas, and leek and stir-fry for 2 minutes, stirring frequently. Add the rice, salt, pepper, soy sauce, and green onions and stir well for 1 minute. Transfer to a large serving platter and garnish with the coriander leaves.

*Serves 4-6.*

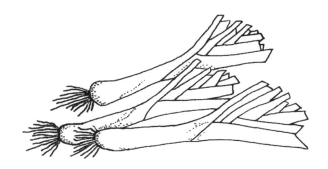

# STIR-FRIED RICE WITH CHICKEN

2 tablespoons canola oil
1 small onion, chopped
4 cloves garlic, minced
1/2 lb. boneless chicken
  breast, thinly sliced
1 small carrot, peeled,
  chopped
1 cup frozen peas
3 cups cooked long-grain
  white rice (see page 129)
1 teaspoon salt
1/2 teaspoon ground
  white pepper
2 tablespoons light soy sauce
4 green onions, chopped

Heat the oil in a large wok and stir-fry the onion and garlic for a few seconds or until light golden brown. Add the chicken and carrot and stir-fry for 3 minutes, stirring frequently. Add the peas, rice, salt, pepper, soy sauce, and green onions and stir-fry for 2 minutes, stirring frequently. Serve hot.

*Serves 4-6.*

# SZECHWAN NOODLES

2 tablespoons canola oil
3 fresh red cayenne
  peppers, sliced
5 cloves garlic, minced
1 lb. ground pork
1/4 cup hot bean sauce
2 tablespoons soy bean
  paste (Miso)
1 tablespoon sugar
1/4 cup light soy sauce
6 green onions, chopped
1 teaspoon sesame oil
1 lb. cooked egg noodles
1 cucumber, peeled, cut
  into julienne strips
2 cups fresh bean sprouts,
  blanched

Heat the oil in a large wok and stir-fry the cayenne peppers, garlic, and pork for 2 minutes, stirring frequently. Add the bean sauce, soy bean paste, sugar, soy sauce, green onions, and sesame oil. Simmer for 10 minutes and set it aside. On a large platter, arrange in layers the cooked noodles, cucumber, and bean sprouts. Pour the pork mixture over it. Serve hot.

*Serves 4-6.*

# DESSERTS

# CHAPTER NINE

## Desserts

# ALMOND COOKIES

1 cup margarine or butter
2/3 cup sugar
2 eggs, beaten
2 teaspoons almond extract
2 cups flour
2/3 cup cornstarch
2 teaspoons baking soda
1/2 teaspoon salt
24 blanched almond halves

Combine the margarine and sugar in a large bowl and beat until creamy. Add 1 egg and the almond extract and beat for a few seconds until well blended. Add the flour, cornstarch, baking soda, and salt and mix with a wooden spoon until the dough is stiff. Roll the dough into 1-inch balls and place them at least 2-inches apart onto oiled cookie sheets. Flatten the cookies slightly and place an almond in the center of each one, pressing down so the dough cracks slightly around the nut. In a small bowl, beat the remaining egg and brush the top of each cookie. Bake in a 350 degree oven for 14 to 16 minutes or until light golden brown. Let the cookies cool on the cookie sheets, then transfer them to a wire rack to cool completely. Serve immediately or store in an airtight container. They will keep for up to 3 weeks.

*Makes 24 cookies.*

# CANDIED BANANAS

1 cup flour, sifted
2 tablespoons cornstarch
1 cup light beer
1 teaspoon canola oil
1 teaspoon vanilla
2 egg whites, stiffly beaten
6 large bananas, peeled,
   cut crosswise diagonally
   into 1-inch thick slices
2 tablespoons Grand Marnier
1 teaspoon finely grated
   orange peel
2 cups canola oil for
   deep-frying
1 cup sugar
3 tablespoons water

In a large bowl, thoroughly mix the flour, cornstarch, beer, oil, and vanilla until it forms a smooth batter. Let it stand at room temperature for at least 30 minutes. Gently fold in the stiffly beaten egg whites. In another large bowl, mix the bananas with Grand Marnier and orange peel. Dip each piece of banana into the batter and deep-fry them in the hot oil for 3 minutes or until golden brown, turning frequently. Remove them from the oil and drain them on paper towels. Bring the sugar and water to a boil in a large pot, stirring constantly. Boil over medium heat for 3 minutes or until the mixture turns light brown and is caramelized. Turn off the heat and add the fried bananas, stirring until well coated on both sides. Place them on a large serving platter and serve immediately.

*Serves 4-6.*

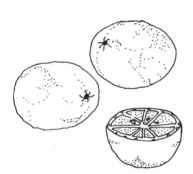

# EIGHT TREASURE RICE PUDDING

1 1/2 cups glutinous rice,
washed, drained
2 cups water
2 tablespoons margarine
5 tablespoons sugar
1 tablespoon canola oil
for brushing the mold
12 Chinese red dates
24 candied lotus seeds
20 brown raisins
20 white raisins
4 pieces candied citron, diced
3 tablespoons candied
orange peel, diced
1/2 cup canned sweet red
bean paste
2/3 cup water
1 tablespoon cornstarch,
dissolved in 1/4 cup of
cold water

In a large, uncovered pot, bring the rice and water to a boil over high heat for 3 minutes, stirring frequently. Lower the heat, cover and simmer for 10 minutes. Add the margarine and 3 tablespoons of sugar and mix well. Set it aside. Brush 1 tablespoon of oil in an 8-inch heat proof bowl and arrange, in circular rows, the Chinese red dates, lotus seeds, brown raisins, white raisins, candied citron, and orange peel. Place 2/3 of the rice mixture in the heat proof bowl, carefully covering the fruit and nuts. Put the red bean paste in the center. Cover with the remaining rice mixture. Place the heatproof bowl in a steamer and steam for 1 hour. Remove the rice pudding from the steamer and invert it onto a serving platter. In a small pot, bring the water to a boil and slowly add the 2 tablespoons of sugar and the cornstarch mixture. Stir well until it thickens slightly. Pour the sauce over the pudding and serve hot or cold.

*Serves 6-8.*

# GLUTINOUS RICE BALLS

1/4 cup sugar
3/4 cup boiling water
2 1/4 cups glutinous rice
  powder
3/4 cup canned sweet red
  bean paste
1 cup sesame seeds
2 cups canola oil for
  deep-frying

In a large bowl, dissolve the sugar in boiling water. Add the rice powder and mix until the dough is well blended. Set it aside. Divide the bean paste into 12 portions and shape each portion into 1-inch balls. Next, flatten the dough into 3-inch circles. Place a bean-paste ball in the center of each 3-inch dough circle. Shape the dough into a ball covering the bean-paste ball. Make sure to seal the edges together. Place the sesame seeds on a cookie sheet and roll the balls onto the sesame seeds. Heat the oil in a large wok and deep-fry the glutinous rice balls, 4 to 6 at a time for 3 minutes each or until light golden brown. Drain them on paper towels. Serve warm.

*Makes 12 balls.*

# GLUTINOUS RICE BALLS WITH COCONUT

2 1/2 cups glutinous
  rice powder
1/4 cup cornstarch
2 tablespoons sugar
1 tablespoon margarine
3/4 cup boiling water
1 cup canned sweet red
  bean paste
1 cup fine dried coconut
  flakes

In a bowl, mix the rice powder, cornstarch, sugar, margarine, and boiling water. Knead the dough until very smooth and soft. Set it aside. Divide the bean paste into 20 portions and shape each portion into 1/2-inch balls. Flatten the dough into 3-inch circles. Place a bean-paste ball in the center of each circle. Shape the dough into a ball covering the bean-paste ball. Be sure to seal the edges. Place them in a steamer on a damp cloth and steam for 10 minutes over high heat. Remove and coat with coconut flakes.

*Makes 20 balls.*

# MANGO GELATIN

1 oz. agar-agar
2 cups warm water
3 cups milk
2/3 cup sugar
1 large ripe mango, peeled,
  seeded, cubed

Soak the agar-agar stick in a large pot with warm water for 1 hour. Add the milk and sugar and bring to a boil over medium heat, stirring constantly or until the agar-agar is completely dissolved. Add the cubed mango and pour it into a 9x13 inch baking dish. Let it stand until completely cool. Refrigerate until the gelatin is firm. Cut into diamond shapes. Serve cold.

*Serves 6-8.*

# Sponge Cake

6 eggs
1 cup sugar
2 cups flour
1 tablespoon baking powder
1 teaspoon baking soda
1/4 cup canola oil
1 teaspoon vanilla
1/2 cup milk
1/2 cup dried candied fruit,
   minced (optional)

Beat the eggs in a large bowl until very stiff. Add the sugar and beat for 5 minutes. Add the flour, baking powder, baking soda, oil, vanilla, milk and candied fruit and mix well with a wooden spoon. Line a 9x13 inch baking dish with wax paper and brush with oil. Pour the batter into the lined baking dish and place it in a steamer. Cover and steam over high heat for 30 minutes. Remove the cake from the steamer. Let the cake cool and remove the wax paper from the bottom of the cake. Cut into squares.

*Serves 4-6.*

# Tofu with Fruit

2 cups fresh orange juice
1 cup crushed rock sugar
   or granulated sugar
1 teaspoon grated
   lemon peel
1 cup canned longans
1 cup canned lychees
1 cup canned peaches,
   cubed
1 cup canned whole
   Mandarin orange
   segments
1 pkg. soft tofu (16 oz.),
   drained, cubed
1 large ripe mango,
   peeled, cubed

Bring the orange juice, rock sugar, and lemon peel to a boil in a medium pot. Reduce the heat to low and simmer for 10 minutes, stirring occasionally or until the sugar dissolves. Remove the pot and let it cool. In a large deep bowl, arrange the longans, lychees, peaches, orange segments, tofu, and mango slices in layers. Pour the orange syrup over the mixed fruit. Chill in a refrigerator before serving.

*Serves 6-8.*

# Cleaning and Scoring Squid

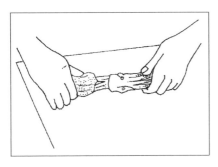

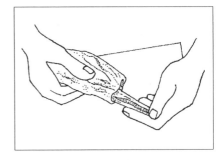

**1.** Pull the tentacles from the body of the squid; the intestines will also come out.

**2.** Pull out the quill from the body.

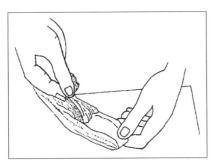

**3.** Peel off the outer skin, rinse out the body and cut the tentacles off at the head.

**4.** Cut to size, depending on the recipe.

# Filling and Wrapping Wontons

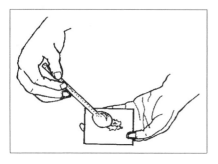

**1.** Place one teaspoonful of the pork mixture in the center of the wrapper.

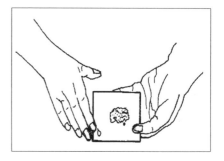

**2.** Wet the edges of the wrapper.

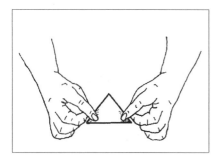

**3.** Fold it up into a triangle by pinching the three corners together.

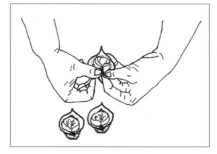

**4.** Wet one of the bottom corners of the triangle and fold it over to overlap the opposite corner and join them by pinching them together.

# Shelling and Deveining Shrimp

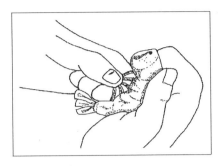

**1.** From the underside of shrimp, remove the legs.

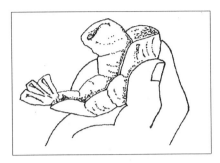

**2.** Roll back the shell from the underside, removing or keeping the tail, as desired.

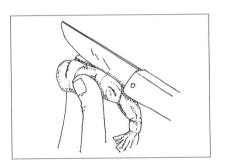

**3.** To devein, cut along the back (not completely through) and remove the vein.

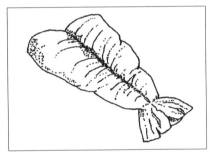

**4.** If butterflying is desired, cut deeper along the back and spread the halves open along the cut in the back.

# Wrapping Spring Rolls

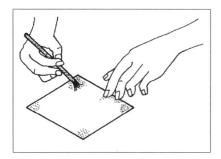

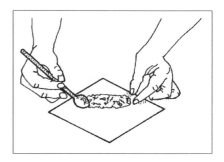

**1.** Place a wrapper with one corner toward you and brush a little egg yolk and water on each corner to seal the spring roll.

**2.** Put two tablespoons of the filling 1/3 of the way from the corner.

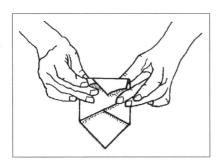

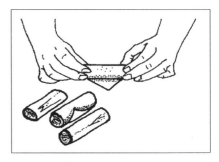

**3.** Fold the closest edge over the filling; then fold the right and left edges.

**4.** Roll up the spring roll, making sure the final edge sticks to the body.

# Suggested Menus

A typical Chinese meal is an array of many different and colorful dishes presented together. Rice is the staple of every meal and tea is usually drunk while savoring the lovely combination of dishes. Below are listed combinations of three menu suggestions which can be enjoyed by you, your family and guests. Try them and share a delightful meal together.

## Quick and Easy Menus

Spinach Salad, page 60
Beef with Bell Peppers, page 105
Asparagus with Baby Corn, page 63

Celery Salad, page 54
Beef with Oyster Sauce, page 108
Eggplant with Chicken, page 69

Spicy Cucumber Salad, page 59
Beef with Black Bean Sauce, page 106
Eggplant with Hot Bean Sauce, page 68

Almond Chicken Salad, page 51
Pork with Black Fungus, page 125
Asparagus with Black Mushrooms, page 63

Bean Sprout Salad, page 53
Beef with Broccoli, page 107
Eggplant with Black Bean Sauce, page 68

Chicken Salad with Mustard, page 55
Spicy Chicken, page 121
Ginger Beef with Pineapple, page 109

# Vegetarian Menus

Stir-Fried Curried Vegetable Rice, page 133
Bean Curd Hot Pot, page 64
Cauliflower Salad, page 54

Mixed Vegetable Pickles, page 13
Bean Curd Sheet Rolls, page 65
Eggplant Salad, page 55

Asparagus Salad, page 52
Szechwan Cucumber Pickles, page 14
Eggplant with Dried Tofu, page 69

Jicama Salad, page 56
Spicy Cabbage, page 72
Stir-Fried Mixed Vegetables, page 77

Lotus Salad, page 57
Buddha's Delight, page 67
Head Lettuce with Oyster Sauce, page 70

Garlic Cucumber Salad, page 56
Stir-Fried Green Beans, page 76
Leek with Bean Curd, page 70

Spinach Soup with Soy Bean Paste, page 45
Lotus with Black Mushrooms, page 71
Spicy Tofu with Black Fungus, page 73

Spinach Tofu Soup, page 45
Spicy Chinese Cabbage Salad, page 59
Stir-Fried Bean Sprouts, page 74

Tomato and Tofu Soup, page 46
Stir-Fried Watercress with Garlic, page 78
Stir-Fried Spinach, page 78

# Elegant Menus

Abalone Soup, page 37
Spicy Shrimp Balls, page 33
Ginger Sauce, page 15
Stuffed Cucumbers, page 80
Shrimp and Snow Pea Salad, page 58
Mongolian Beef, page 110
Candied Bananas, page 138

Chicken and Asparagus Soup, page 38
Deep-Fried Chicken Wings, page 27
Steamed Clams with Ginger, page 85
Pickled Szechwan Salad, page 57
Scallops with Black Mushrooms, page 94
Eight Treasure Rice Pudding, page 139

Creamy Crab Corn Soup, page 41
Barbecued Pork, page 23
Hot Mustard Sauce, page 17
Clams with Black Bean Sauce, page 84
Sweet and Sour Shrimp, page 100
Glutinous Rice Balls with Coconut, page 141

Wintermelon Soup, page 47
Chicken Spring Rolls, page 24
Crab with Baby Bok Choy, page 86
Shrimp with Black Bean Sauce, page 97
Crispy Roast Duck, page 122
Mango Gelatin, page 141

Hot and Sour Soup, page 42
Steamed Spareribs, page 34
Abalone with Black Mushrooms, page 83
Stir-Fried Chinese Cabbage, page 75
Scallops with Mixed Vegetables, page 95
Fried Fish with Black Bean Sauce, page 87
Tofu with Fruit, page 142

# Essential Ingredients

Agar-Agar
Bean Curd Sheet
Canned Abalone
Canned Baby Corn
Canned Bamboo Shoots
Canned Straw Mushrooms
Canned Sweet Red Bean Paste
Canned Water Chestnuts
*Canola Oil
Cashew Nuts
Cellophane Noodles
Chili Sauce
Chinese Cabbage
Chinese Five-Spice Powder
Curry Powder
Dried Black Chinese Mushrooms
Dried Black Fungus
Dried Plums
Dried Shrimp
Flavored Dried Tofu
Fresh Coriander Leaves
Ginger
Glutinous Rice
Grand Marnier
Hoisin Sauce
Hot Bean Sauce

Hot Mustard Powder
Japanese Eggplant
Jicama
Light Soy Sauce
Lili Buds
Lotus Root
Oyster Sauce
Rice Vermicelli
Rice Vinegar
Rice Wine
Rock Sugar
Salted Chinese Black Beans
Sesame Oil
Sesame Seeds
Shallots
Soy Bean Paste
Spring Roll Wrappers
Star Anise
Szechwan Peppercorns
Tapioca Flour
Tofu (Soy Bean Curd)
Watercress
White Glutinous Rice
White Icicle Radish
Wintermelon
Yuba Sticks

*Any kind of oil may be used; however, for better cooking results and for health concerns, I use and recommend the following: for deep-frying, use a refined, high oleic, monounsaturated safflower oil (Spectrum Naturals) or canola oil; for stir-frying, use unrefined, high oleic, monounsaturated safflower oil (Spectrum Naturals) or canola oil. Safflower oil is available in health food stores; canola oil is readily available in supermarkets. In China, peanut oil, corn oil, soya oil, cottonseed oil, vegetable oil, and sesame oil are usually used.

# Glossary

**ABALONE:** A large mollusk with an ear-shaped shell. It has a rubbery texture and is usually available in cans in Asian markets.

**AGAR-AGAR:** Also called *kanten* in Japanese. A form of seaweed gelatin available in threads, squares, and powdered. It is completely colorless and tasteless, and it sets without refrigeration. Widely used in Asia and available in Asian markets.

**BABY CORN:** Crunchy yellow-colored young miniature corn on the cob which averages 3 to 4 inches length. Available in cans in Asian markets.

**BAMBOO SHOOTS:** A crisp, cream-colored, conical-shaped vegetable used frequently in all Asian cooking. It is much simpler to buy the canned variety which is readily available in all Asian and many Western markets.

**BLACK CHINESE MUSHROOMS:** Although sold dried, they must be soaked in warm water for some time before using. The hard stems are discarded. Available in Asian and Western markets.

**BLACK FUNGUS:** (Wood Fungus) Available both whole and in strips; however, they must be soaked in warm water for 10 minutes before using. They are bland with a crunchy texture, having little taste of their own, but taking on the flavor of whatever they are cooked with. Available in Asian markets.

**CANDIED LOTUS SEEDS:** Sweet, dried, white seeds with a nut-like flavor similar to chestnuts. Available in Asian markets.

**CANNED SWEET RED BEAN PASTE:** Tiny, red beans cooked with butter, sugar, and vanilla extract. Properly puréed through a fine sieve to remove the coarse outer skin, it is used as a filling for both sweet and savory treats. Available in Asian markets.

**CASHEW NUTS:** Sweet, kidney-shaped nuts, available raw, roasted, or salted in most markets.

**CAYENNE PEPPERS:** Very hot peppers, available fresh or dried in most markets.

**CELLOPHANE NOODLES:** Also known as "bean thread vermicelli," a firm transparent noodle made from mung beans. They are usually soaked in warm water for 5 minutes before using. They are also deep-fried straight from the packet when used as a garnish or salad. Available in Asian and Western markets.

**CHILI SAUCE:** (Chinese Style) A hot sauce made from fresh cayenne peppers, salt and vinegar. Available in Asian markets.

**CHINESE CABBAGE:** (Napa Cabbage) A sweet and mild cabbage whose pale green or yellowish leaves are firm and tightly packed. Available in most markets.

**CHINESE FIVE-SPICE POWDER:** A combination of ground star anise, licorice root, cinnamon, cloves, fennel, and ground black pepper. It is a very strong seasoning and should be used sparingly. Available in most markets.

**DRIED COCONUT FLAKES:** Peeled, ground, dehydrated coconut meat with a delicate sweet flavor. It is available unsweetened in health food stores and Asian markets.

**DRIED SHRIMP:** A small, peeled, delicately sweet-flavored shrimp, dehydrated by the sun or air-dried. Available in Asian markets.

**FLAVORED DRIED TOFU:** A weight is placed on freshly made tofu (Bean Curd) to squeeze out excess liquid. The tofu is marinated in soy sauce, sugar, star anise, and spices. It tastes like and has the texture of smoked meat. Available in 10.5 oz. packages in Asian markets.

**FRESH CORIANDER LEAVES:** Also known as cilantro and Chinese parsley, it has a very distinctive flavor. Available in most markets. No substitute.

**GINGER:** A smooth-skinned, buff-colored root, used both for seasoning dishes and as a condiment. Available fresh in most markets.

**GLUTINOUS RICE:** A long-grained variety of rice known as sticky-rice or sweet rice. It is used frequently for rice desserts. Available in Asian markets.

**GRAND MARNIER:** French orange liqueur available in stores where hard liquor is sold.

**HOISIN SAUCE:** A sweet, reddish-brown, thick sauce made from soy bean paste, garlic, sugar, and spices. Available in Asian markets.

**HOT BEAN SAUCE:** (Chinese Style) It is a smooth mixture of ground yellow bean, chili sauce, sugar, salt and spices. Available in Asian markets.

**HOT MUSTARD POWDER:** A pungent, fiery-flavored condiment often served with deep-fried appetizers. Dried powder and prepared mustard in jars are found in Asian markets.

**JAPANESE EGGPLANT:** Six to ten inches long and about two inches in diameter, this eggplant is very tasty and tender. Available in Asian and Western markets.

**JICAMA:** Usually thought of as a Mexican vegetable, jicama is a tuber common in Southeast Asia as well. Its availability and character make it a great substitute for fresh water chestnuts. It must be peeled before being used in a recipe. It has a sweet flavor and crunchy texture. Available in most markets.

**LILY BUDS:** Very nutritious, long, narrow, dried golden buds with a very delicate flavor, they must be soaked in warm water for 20 minutes prior to use. Discard the hard stem ends and tie each bud in a knot, especially for soups. Available in Asian markets.

**LOTUS ROOT:** Pale brown stem of the water lily which looks like potatoes that are attached to each other. It varies in size, and when peeled and sliced crosswise, reveals an interesting cross-section showing the air holes that run the length of the root. Lotus root adds a delicate sweetness and a fibrous crunch to salads, soups, and braised dishes. Available in Asian markets.

**OYSTER SAUCE:** Made from oysters cooked in salted water and soy sauce. It keeps well and adds a delicate flavor to meat and vegetable dishes. Rrefrigerate the bottle after opening. Available in most markets.

**RICE VERMICELLI:** Thin, white noodles made from rice flour. Available in most markets.

**RICE WINE:** (Chinese Shao Xing Rice Wine Brand) A rich amber-colored liquid made from a blend of glutinous rice, millet, yeast, and spring water. Traditionally, it was aged 10 to 100 years to achieve its rich full-bodied flavor. Dry sherry can be substituted but cannot equal the rich, mellow taste of rice wine. Available in most markets.

**ROCK SUGAR:** Pale amber-colored crystals made from a combination of refined and unrefined sugars and honey. When used to make sauce, you may need to break the lumps into smaller pieces with a wooden mallet or rolling pin. Available in Asian markets.

**SALTED BLACK BEANS:** A highly flavorful ingredient made from black soy beans which have been cooked and fermented. Used to season meat, chicken and seafood. Available in Asian stores in cans or plastic bags.

**SESAME OIL:** Extracted from toasted sesame seeds, it is widely used in Oriental cooking in small quantities for flavoring. Available in Asian and Western markets.

**SESAME SEEDS:** Small flat seeds used as a source of oil and as a garnish. Available in Asian and Western markets.

**SHALLOTS:** Small, purplish sweet onions with red-brown skin. Available in Asian and Western markets.

**SOY BEAN PASTE:** (Miso) A paste of fermented soy beans, cereal grain and salt. Available in Asian markets and in the gourmet food sections of supermarkets.

**SOY SAUCE:** (Shoyu) A sauce made from fermented and processed soy beans, salt, and wheat in water. Available in most markets.

**SPRING ROLL WRAPPERS:** Thin white wrappers made from flour, water, and salt. Sold in plastic packets and kept frozen. Thaw and peel off one at a time (unused wrappers can be re-frozen). Available in Asian markets.

**STAR ANISE:** Dried, star-shaped spice of an evergreen tree native to China, it has a licorice flavor and should be stored in a tightly sealed jar. Available in Asian markets.

**STRAW MUSHROOMS:** Usually canned, they have a delicate flavor and chewy texture. Available in Asian markets.

**SZECHWAN PEPPERCORNS:** Dried reddish brown berries that add a woodsy fragrance and leave a pleasantly numbing feeling in the mouth. They should be roasted before grinding to bring out their full flavor. Available in Asian markets.

**TAPIOCA FLOUR:** Ground cassava root used for desserts and as a thickening agent in cooking. Available in Asian markets.

**TOFU:** (Soy Bean Curd) A soft white curd which is made from soy beans and resembles fresh white cheese. It is bland, having little taste of its own, but taking on the flavor of whatever it is cooked with. It is high in protein and low in calories; it is low in saturated fat and is cholesterol-free. It is also rich in vitamins and minerals. Four kinds of tofu are widely available (Soft, Medium, Firm, and Extra Firm) and are sold in plastic containers which are transparent on top. Each container of tofu weighs 10 to 16 ounces. Available in Asian and Western markets.

**WATERCRESS:** Dark green in color with glossy leaves, it has a hot peppery flavor. Available in most markets.

**WATER CHESTNUTS:** Usually canned, but occasionally found fresh, water chestnuts have a crunchy texture. When fresh, their brown skin must be peeled off with a sharp knife and discarded. Available in most markets.

**WHITE ICICLE RADISH:** (Daikon) A long white, sweet radish native to Japan, it is often served grated with deep-fried, oily foods, as it is considered an aid to digestion. Available in Asian and health food stores.

**WINTERMELON:** Resembling a watermelon, its skin is dark green, while its interior is greenish white with white seeds. It has the characteristic of absorbing the flavors of whatever it is cooked with. Available in Asian markets.

**YUBA STICKS:** (Dried Bean Curd) A nutritious and very high proteined soy food that forms when boiling soy milk, made by rolling the skin into sticks and drying. Available in most markets.

# Index

# S

# T

# V

# W

# Truly **Ambrosia**

## Delightful Chinese Cooking

## Delightful Tofu Cooking

## Delightful Vietnamese Cooking

## Delightful Brazilian Cooking

## Delightful Thai Cooking

coming soon

## Delightful Italian Cooking

## Delightful Vegetarian Cooking

## Delightful Indonesian Cooking

# Ordering Information

Please send me:

| | |
|---|---|
| _____copies of Delightful Chinese Cooking, $13.95 | $_____ |
| _____copies of Delightful Tofu Cooking, $12.95 | $_____ |
| _____copies of Delightful Vietnamese Cooking, $12.95 | $_____ |
| _____copies of Delightful Brazilian Cooking, $14.95 | $_____ |
| _____copies of Delightful Thai Cooking, $12.95 | $_____ |
| _____set of 5 copies, $50.00 a set | $_____ |

**Shipping & Handling:**

| | |
|---|---|
| $3.00 first copy | $_____ |
| $1.00 each additional copy | $_____ |
| Set of five $7.00 each set | $_____ |

Washingt

**Payment**

❑   Che

**Mail Pa**

**Ship Or**

Name__

Address

City__

State__

❑Autog